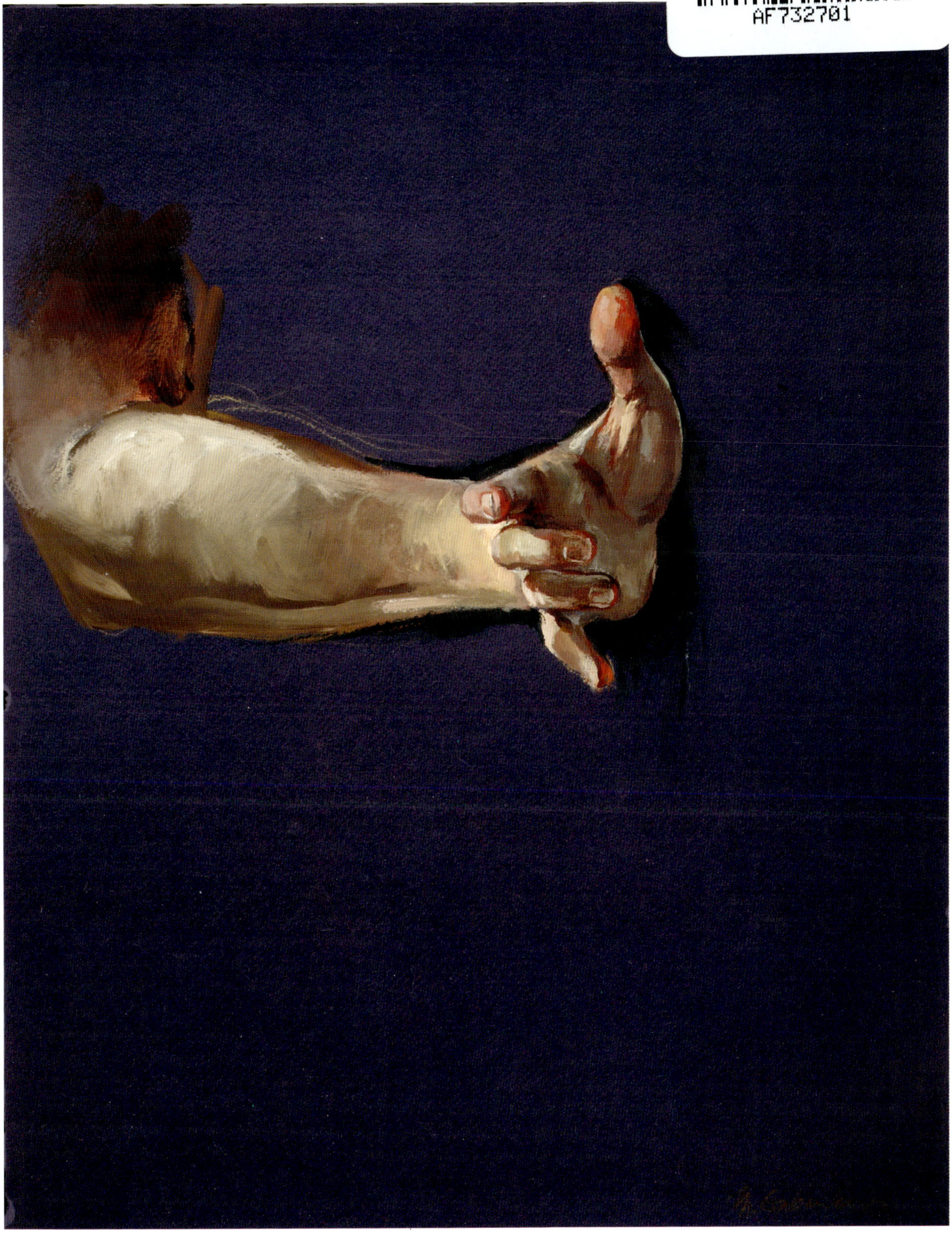

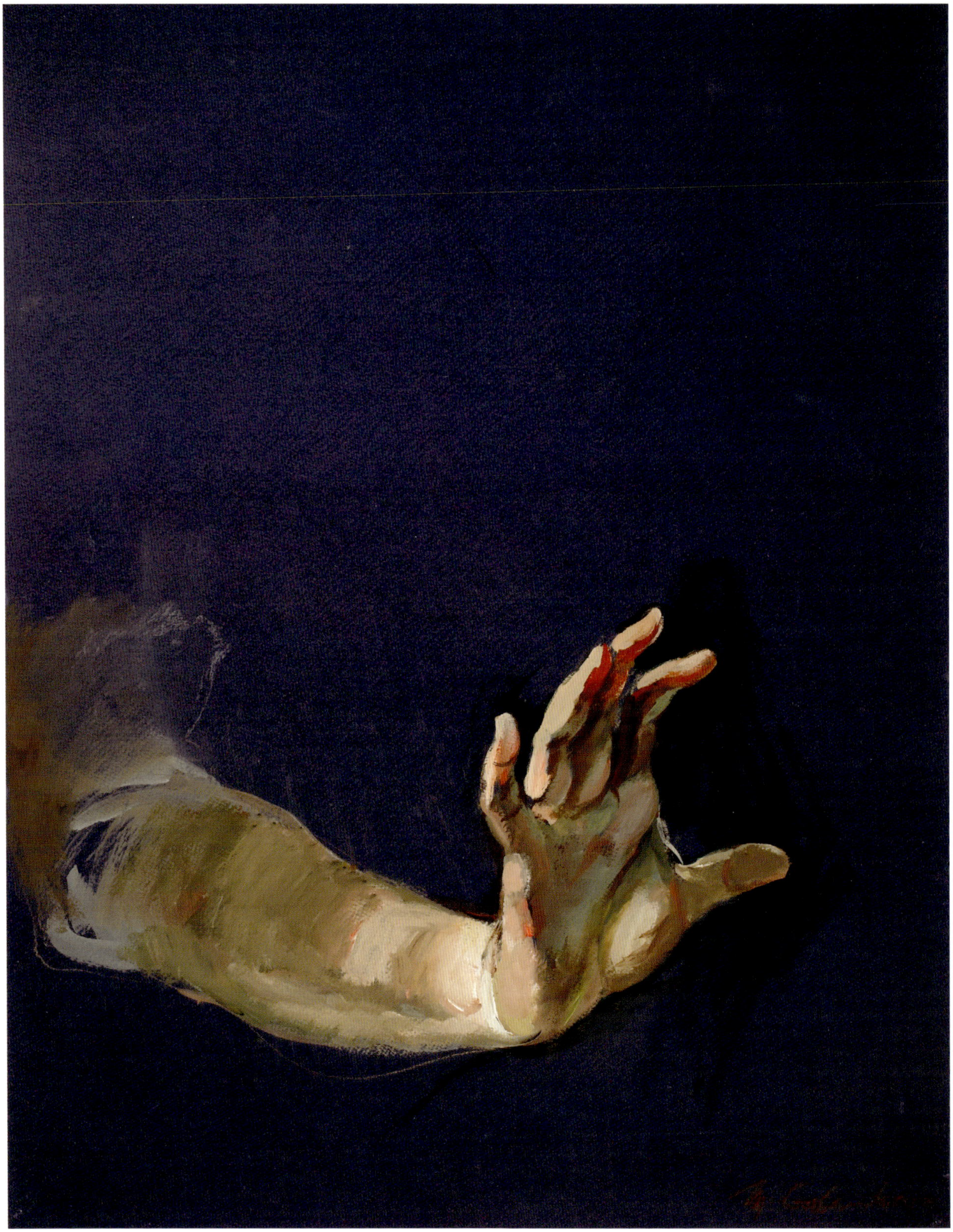

Body Broken—Body Redeemed
The Art of Maria Gabankova

With an Introduction by John Franklin

Soli Deo Gloria

PIQUANT editions

This book is dedicated to my parents, Antonia Lanik Gabanek and Joseph Gabanek, and my brother, Jan Gabanek.

I would like to express my deep gratitude to my husband, Aleš Březina, on whose skills, support and patience I relied through all stages of work in the creation of this book. My sincere thanks for their support are also due to Catherine Beaudette, Janice Cermak, Adrienne Dengerink Chaplin, Lois Ellis Lawson, John Franklin, Vladyana Krykorka, Jack Johnson, Elria and Pieter Kwant, Yvonne Nowicka-Wright and Barbora Stelzl.

Maria Gabankova
Toronto, 2007

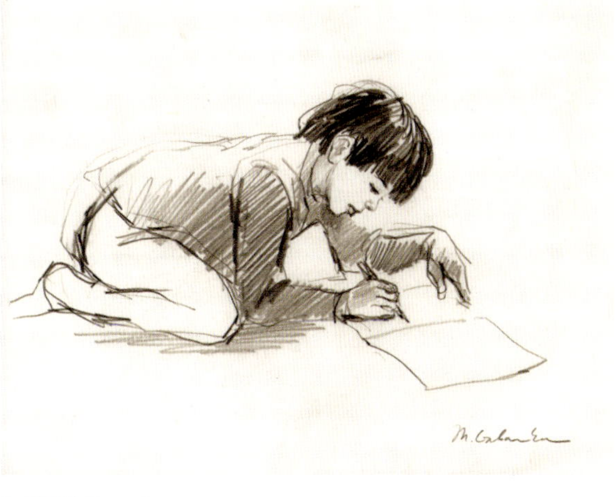

A Child Drawing

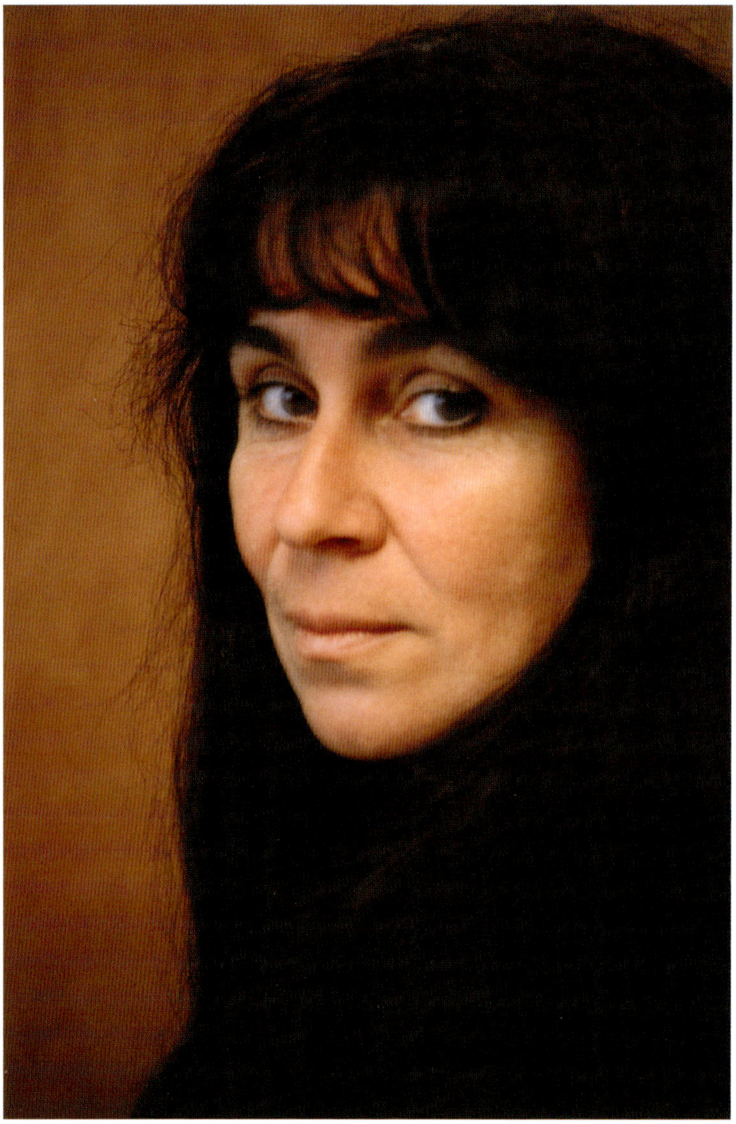

Maria Gabankova
Photograph by Joseph Gabanek

Probing the Mystery: The Art of Maria Gabankova

Both artists and scientists have long been fascinated by the human body, the place where time and eternity, flesh and spirit meet in the mystery we call humanity. The links between anatomy and the visual arts have a long history. Perhaps the most famous work illustrating this connection is a painting by Rembrandt of *The Anatomy Lesson of Dr Nicholaes Tulp* (1632): 'The picture oscillates ... between a pessimistic and optimistic spectrum of meaning. At one end of the spectrum, we are asked to reflect on our own mortality, whilst at the other end, we are urged, nevertheless, to celebrate the wisdom of God who has reserved for humanity a special place in creation.' [1] The work found in this book resonates with these themes.

Attention to the human figure was largely lost in the twentieth century as artists turned to works of abstraction, installation pieces and a general commitment to conceptual art driven by self-expression. But the interest in the human figure did not completely disappear. In America, Philip Pearlstein produced near-photographic likenesses; in England, there was the ever-solemn and at times unsettling work of Francis Bacon, and the raw realism of Lucien Freud; and in Canada there was the magic realism of Alex Colville. Recently other visual artists have been paying attention to the human figure. This group includes artists of Christian faith such as Bruce Hermann, Ed Knippers and Tim Lowly in America, and in Canada, Erica Grimm-Vance, Gerald Folkerts, David Robinson—and Maria Gabankova. Gabankova's career-long commitment to figurative art manifests the influence of her great European predecessors. But her fascination with the human figure is rooted in the belief that gestures and emotions are powerful tools for expressing ideas and discovering insights.

Maria Gabankova's sensibilities were deeply shaped by her early environment. She was born in Czechoslovakia when it was still under a communist regime. Her father was an artist, but also a conscientious objector and a political prisoner at the end of the Stalinist era. After the Soviet-led invasion of Czechoslovakia by the Warsaw Pact armies in 1968, her parents, Antonia Lanik Gabanek and Joseph Gabanek, left their homeland and emigrated to Canada with their two children, Maria and Jan. Both of Maria's parents are figure painters, and her own interest in this field developed early. The work and encouragement of her parents and the training and experience she received while studying at the Art Students League of New York enabled her to pursue this interest, despite pressure to follow the popular trends in the 1970s of turning to conceptual art and self-expression.

Religious faith began to stir in Gabankova in her early twenties, and she began to pay more careful attention to the wonder of God's creation. Art historian Hans Rookmaaker's book *The Creative Gift* encouraged her by providing insight into how being a Christian and a contemporary artist need not be in conflict. She followed her artistic calling with the spirit captured in Leonardo Da Vinci's words: 'For painting is a way to learn to know the Maker of all marvellous things—and this is the way to love so great an inventor.'[2] Evident in her work is a sense of joy, wonder and discovery as she observes the natural world and specifically the human body.

Narrative characterizes Gabankova's paintings, and we are invited to participate in these deeply personal vignettes on canvas. The work you will find in this book is personal in two ways. It is born out of the rich and indelible experiences of the life of the artist, which speak to the stark realities of our world, and it is personal in its attention to the human condition in all its complexity. Gabankova is always aware that we may not *see* what we are *looking at*, and that both life and art call us to an engaging gaze if we are to see below the surface of things. Through her art, she seeks to gain glimpses of the meaning of ordinary objects, and most particularly of the meaning of human existence.

Gabankova is an astute observer of human beings, both in the physical world of flesh and blood and in the internal realm of the spirit. The individual portrayed in her paintings is not the self-sufficient individual of modern Western culture but rather the individual isolated, vulnerable and alone, longing for something more.

[1] Jonathan Sawday, *The Body Emblazoned: Dissection and the Human Body in Renaissance Culture*, (London: Routledge, 1995) p151

[2] Leonardo da Vinci, *Notebooks of Leonardo da Vinci* (Oxford University Press, 1998) p217

This is art that unmasks the pretence and hubris that so often attend human behaviour. It is art that protests against the dehumanizing influences that plague us: the violence, destruction and despair that attend the deep divisions in our social, political and religious landscape, the battles that rage around us and within us.

Gabankova's work is philosophical; it looks for the deeper meaning of life. It probes beyond the fragmentations common to postmodern culture and searches for coherence and harmony. It acknowledges the truth about our existence as fragile and vulnerable; yet, the pain and suffering that afflict body and spirit are illuminated by a reassuring ray which sustains hope amidst the darkness of life. There is a play of light and shadow in her depictions of the human figure that evokes not only what is seen with the eye but also what is experienced in the soul.

Body Broken—Body Redeemed illustrates how Gabankova brings together the reality of human brokenness and the hope of human redemption. The work collected here avoids the polarities of nihilism and triumphalism. Much of contemporary art leads us into a cul-de-sac from which there is no escape. While, too often, the art found in religious settings is triumphalistic, naïve in its inclination to pander to our desire for joyful harmony while neglecting or perhaps avoiding the chaos of human brokenness and the dark side of our individual and social realities. Gabankova's approach resonates with the biblical story which offers us a holistic understanding of humanity, refusing the temptations of both nihilism and triumphalism. Instead, it reveals the same sort of oscillation seen in Rembrandt's painting—the oscillation between human mortality and immortality, the dialectic of life and death.

But in addition to this, Gabankova's paintings also express the fuzzy lines between the real and unreal. The figures in *Report from a Leaky Boat* (p26) and *Freedombound* (p20) exist on the threshold between living flesh and static, lifeless mannequins. The *Leaky Boat* echoes *The Ship of Fools* by Hieronymus Bosch

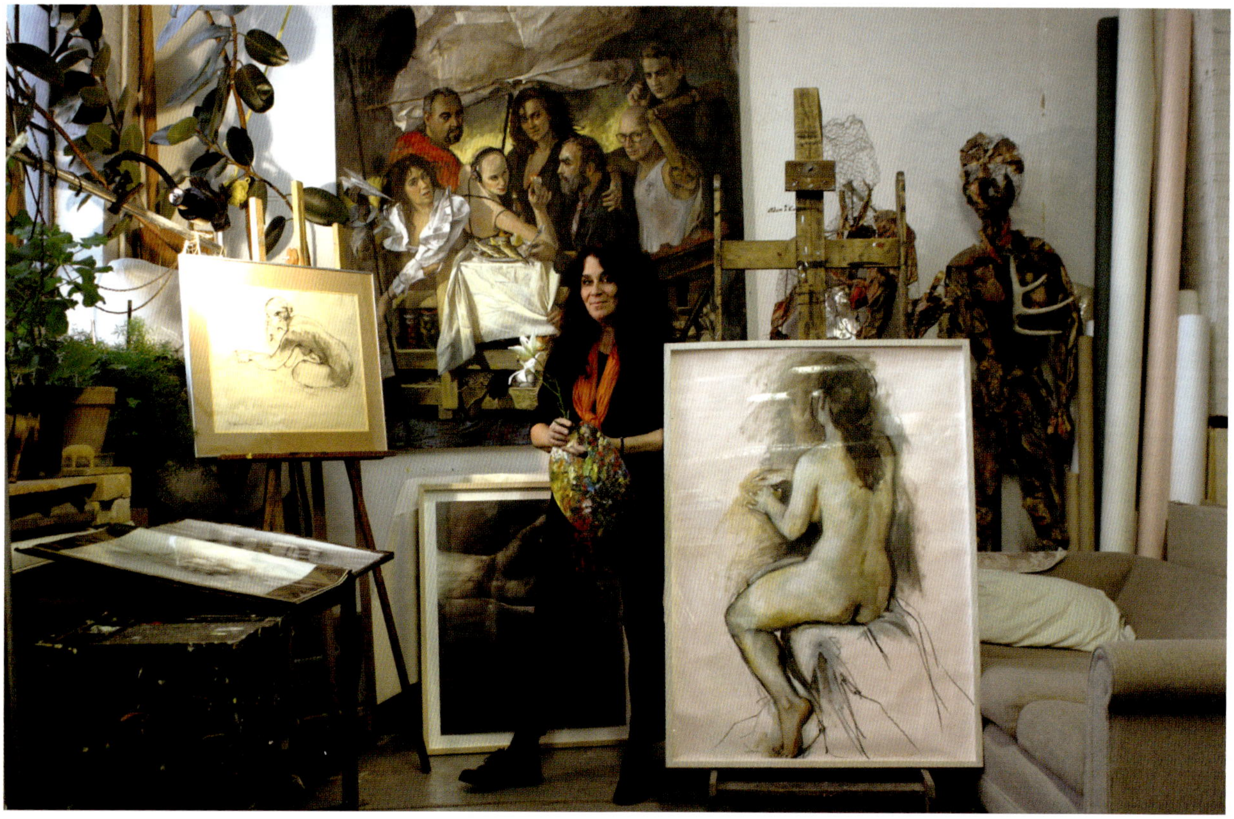

In the Toronto Studio (Photo: M Babel)

(1450–1516). The theme of an aimless voyage accompanied by self-indulgent play resonates in a postmodern culture. *Freedombound* provides us with a telling metaphor for a superficial understanding of freedom which is ultimately self-destructive. In the self-portrait *The Joker's New Clothes* (p24) the mixture of animate and inanimate in the figure leaves us unsure whether the joker's dance disregards or celebrates the technology that surrounds her.

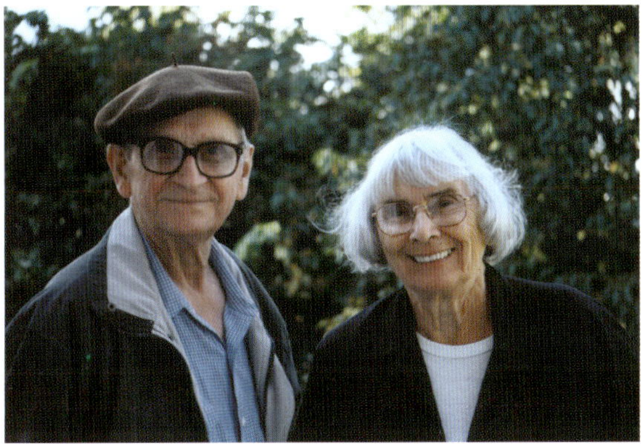

Artist's parents, Joseph Gabanek and Antonia Lanik Gabanek

Society's current concern with 'body image' focuses purely on surface appearances. Gabankova's anatomical paintings, however, take us below the surface and disclose the bones, organs, arteries and veins that make our bodies what they are. These works challenge the false glamour of contemporary self-understandings and remind us of our vulnerability and of the wonder of the body's intricacies. And in a surprising way, Gabankova takes this 'inside' view of the body as the means of depicting an image of *The Cross* (p16): flesh and blood—broken for the sake of all humanity.

The bold and surreal paintings of *Hammer in the Head* (p40) and *Globalization* (p41) have an arresting impact. At first it is difficult to discern what one is looking at, but soon the picture comes clear and we are left with stark and disturbing representations of the state of our society and of individuals. The unsettling reflection depicted in *Selfportrait—Fear* (p42) could be an icon for how many in our world experience life. *The Fall* (p37) suggests the chaos and vulnerability of the human condition as bodies float downward with no apparent capacity to control their fall, while their flesh seems to undergo a transformation. All this is accompanied by the sinister presence of the face of evil—a satanic figure.

Another aspect of the brokenness addressed in Gabankova's work is our failures of compassion. *Forgotten News* (p12) vividly shows how easily pain, suffering and tragedy become yesterday's news. Famine, poverty, war, homelessness, violence and oppression are set aside in a pile to be recycled while we await the next wave of information. The faceless figure prompts us to remember how quickly we can become immune to the stark realities of life, whether half a world away or on the streets of our own town. *Kosovo* (p19) can be read as a lament for a war-torn country where the innocent suffer while those in power work out their ill-advised plans. Within the blood-red cloak we see gentle compassionate hands and the pained and almost prayerful face of a young woman carrying some of the weight of the surrounding conflict. The drawing series *Sleeper I, II and III* (pp8–10) manifests a compassionate gaze on figures weary from the weight of life's demands and the diminished strength of an aging body. We are drawn to these simple figures bent by the cares of life, and are made grateful for the gift of sleep.

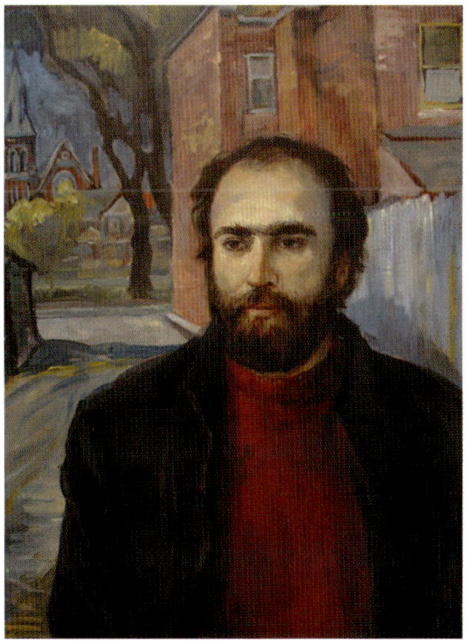

Artist's husband, Aleš Březina

Gabankova's work plays on paradox: what is depicted points to its opposite. Our awareness of brokenness becomes the means through which our need for redemption is disclosed. In these paintings we are not left to despair but find, instead, a breaking in of hope with the promise of a *body redeemed*. There is no magical escape from the human condition, only signs that this is not all there is.

Undergirding the work is the artist's conviction that the spiritual is revealed through the physical. The spirituality woven into her imagery is not a disembodied spirituality but one which accepts the material world as a gift of the divine artist who has created all things. The transforming power of faith is captured in the painting titled *Psalms* (p50). In this work she juxtaposes word and image, drawing on the rich resources of the biblical psalms. While praying, the kneeling figure is being changed from mere stone to flesh and blood. Just beside the feet of this figure are words from Psalm 119—'Thy word is a lamp unto my feet'. The Bible serves as a foundation that grounds and shapes the perspective informing all of Gabankova's work. Her art is never preachy, but it is saturated in the biblical narrative. *Hope* (p46) provides another image where the sacred text with its well-worn pages can be seen as a resource for ordinary life.

We should not overlook the cleverly constructed heads, part of a series of seven titled *Special Department (Paper Head I* and *II*, pp22, 23). These well-executed paintings are full of humour and make us laugh a little at ourselves. But humour, as one author put it, is a signal of transcendence; it suggests to us that there is more in life than meets the eye, more than the collection of my experiences. Humour gives us a sense that hope is not futile. A glimpse of this hope is found in *Waiting for a Miracle* (p52). The foot washing in this painting takes place across social boundaries, indicating our call to be servants to one another and not to be deterred by social expectations or by our differences. In the unclothed bodies of the two main figures, where the emotions are much more in view, the artist captures the joy and gentleness of the giver, while uncertainty and even a sense of being undeserving can be seen in the face of the receiver. Those who witness this act of service seem almost oblivious to what is happening—and appear to have little concern for its depth of meaning. It is easy to miss the meaningful in ordinary life.

Messenger 1 and *2* (pp30, 32) are two examples from a series inspired by the biblical book of Revelation. These are no sentimentalized angels; they are assertive young women clasping trumpets that they are ready to sound to awaken us from our complacent self-indulgence and alert us to the divine judgment on human disobedience. These images hint at human accountability and suggest that what we do in time may have implications for eternity.

In *Messengers of Light* (p48) we are reminded that the body broken can become the body redeemed because of the resurrection of Jesus. Here is where light comes to dispel darkness, where despair is overcome by hope, and where we find the promise that brokenness will be transformed into wholeness. This same promise is eloquently expressed in *New Song* (p56), where those gathered around the table are participants in a fellowship, joined together by common faith as beneficiaries of the work accomplished by 'the Lamb of God who takes away the sin of the world'. Musical instruments are there to speak praises to God, while food and drink symbolize a celebration of the richness of divine provision. This image focuses our gaze on a promised future, one that we can catch glimpses of in the present. These works express the hope that one day all things will be made new.

This book contains only a selection of Gabankova's work, for within her repertoire of painting you can find still-lifes, architectural studies and portraits. The art found in these pages are strong works, bold, compelling, insightful and deeply spiritual. They serve as windows into the mystery of human existence and the mystery of human salvation. There is a prophetic thread in these paintings, not a self-conscious one, but one that emerges from the integrity of the work and of the artist as she seeks to depict the drama of the human spirit in the struggle for meaning and significance. Born of a sense of wonder and a hopeful spirit, these paintings invite us to look afresh at what it means to be human. Despite the darkness in life, they call us to nurture a spirit of hope. In this rich collection of visual art we sense that life is not a possession to be grasped but a gift to be received, a miracle that inspires gratitude.

John Franklin

John Franklin has lectured in theology and philosophy. At present he is the Executive Director of Imago, a registered charity that promotes the work of Christians in the arts in Canada (www.imago-arts.on.ca). He is also the editor of the quarterly Imago Newsletter. John is based in Toronto.

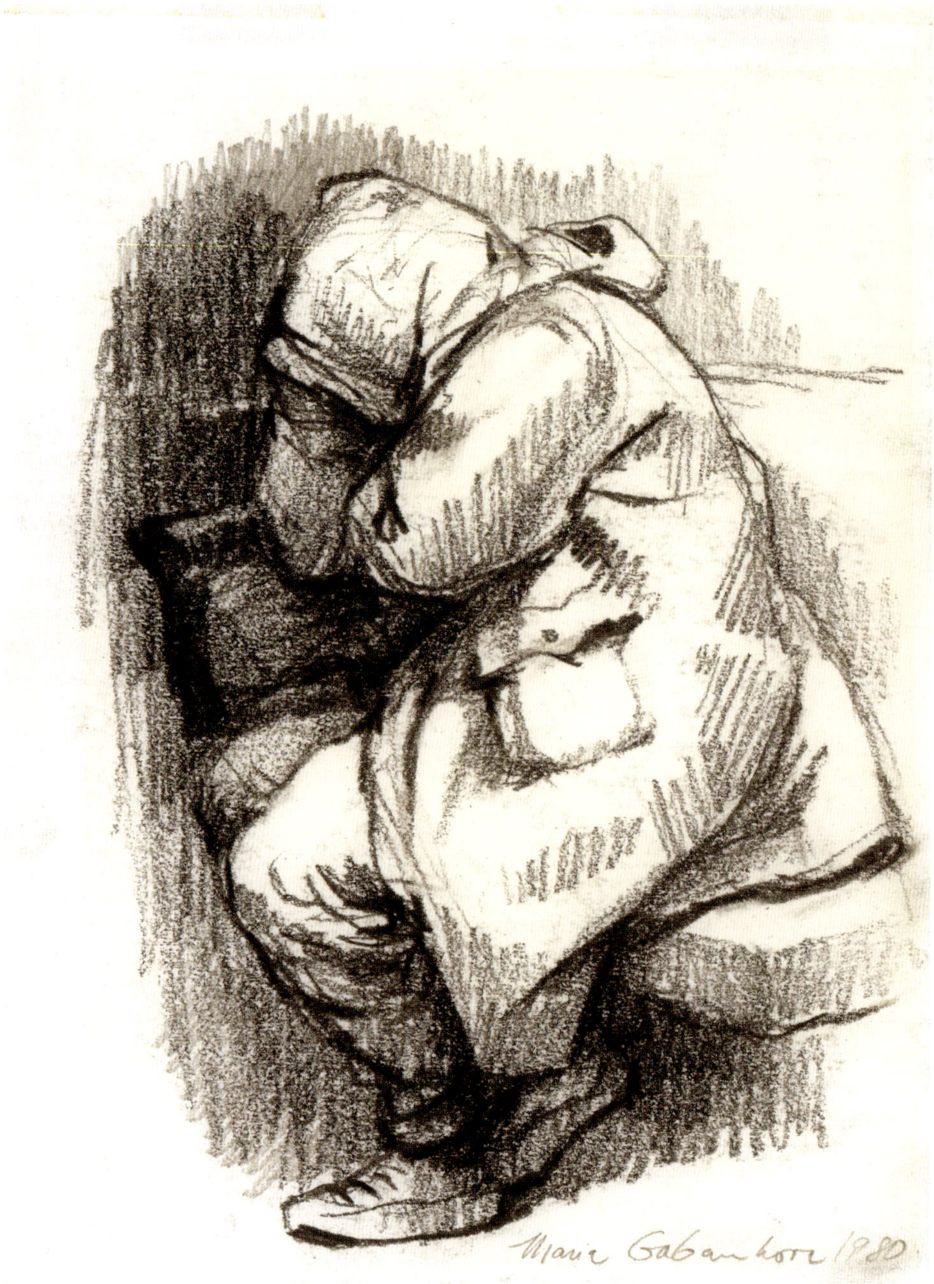

Sleeper II

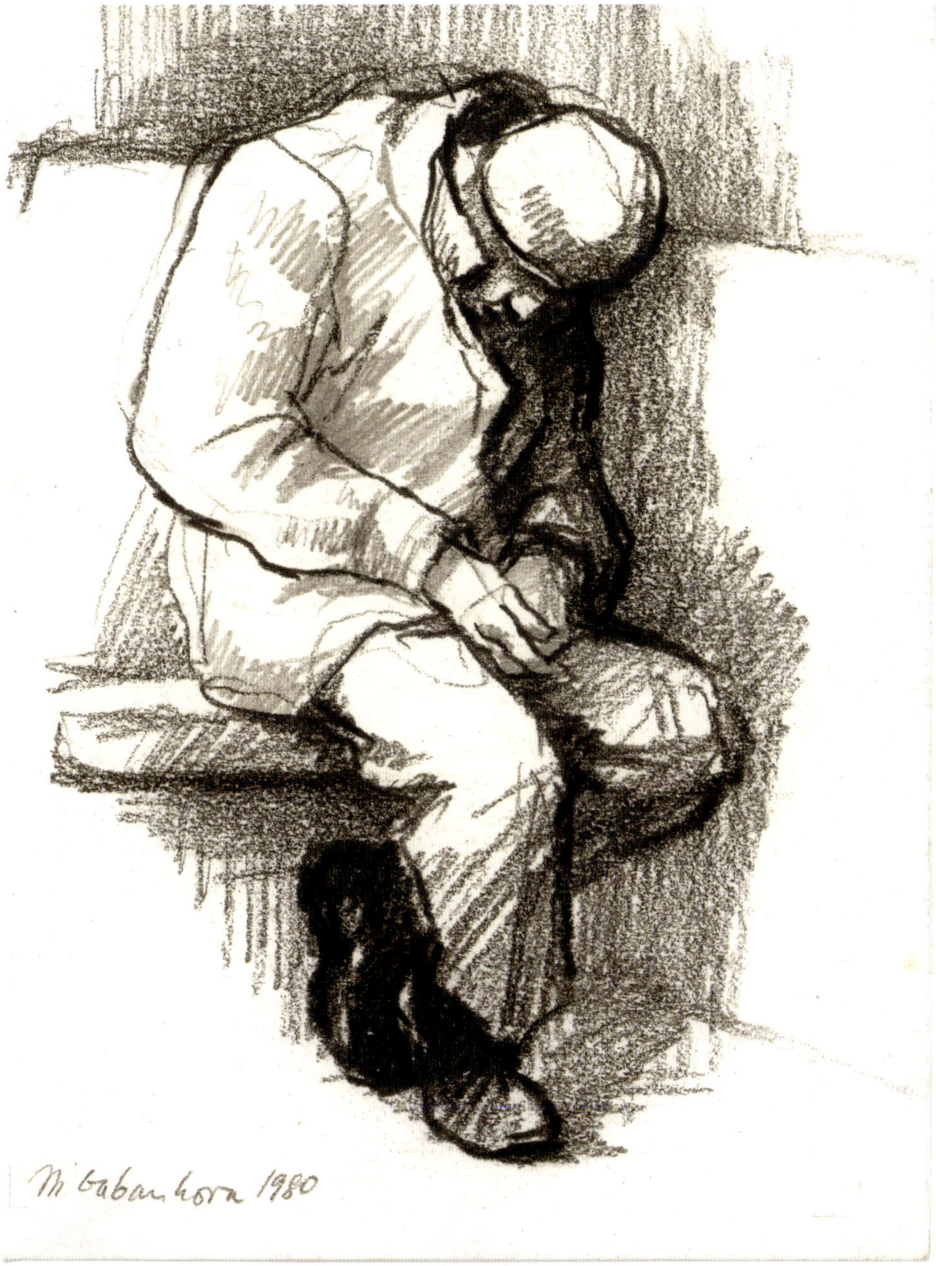

Sleeper I

These drawings from life were done on the New York subway in 1980, during commutes from Queens to Manhattan, where I studied at the Art Students League. At times I would even travel a few stops past my destination in order to finish a drawing. Many homeless persons lived on the city streets and the subway. I was deeply moved by the vulnerability of their body positions, with their faces often obscured.

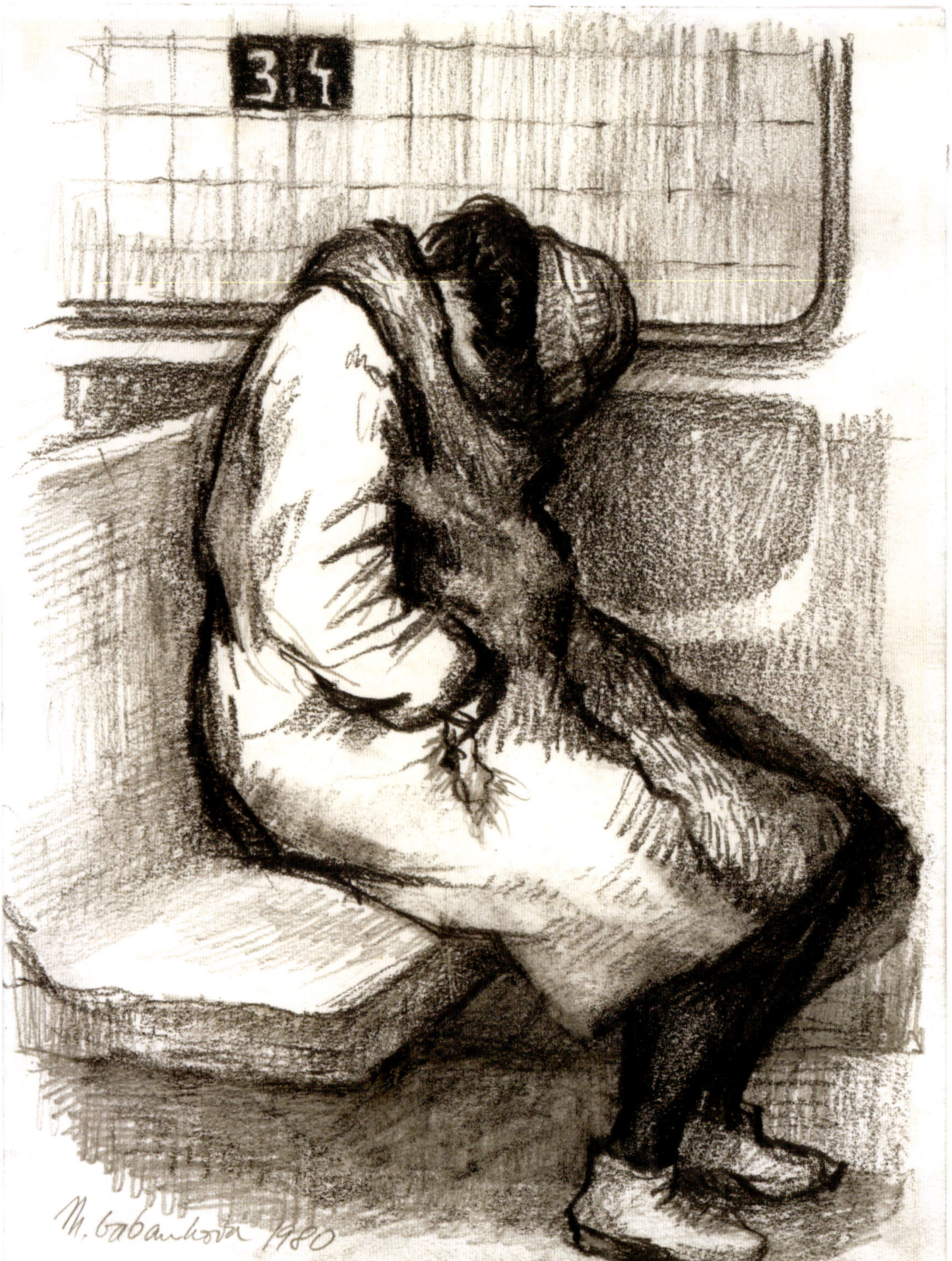

Sleeper III

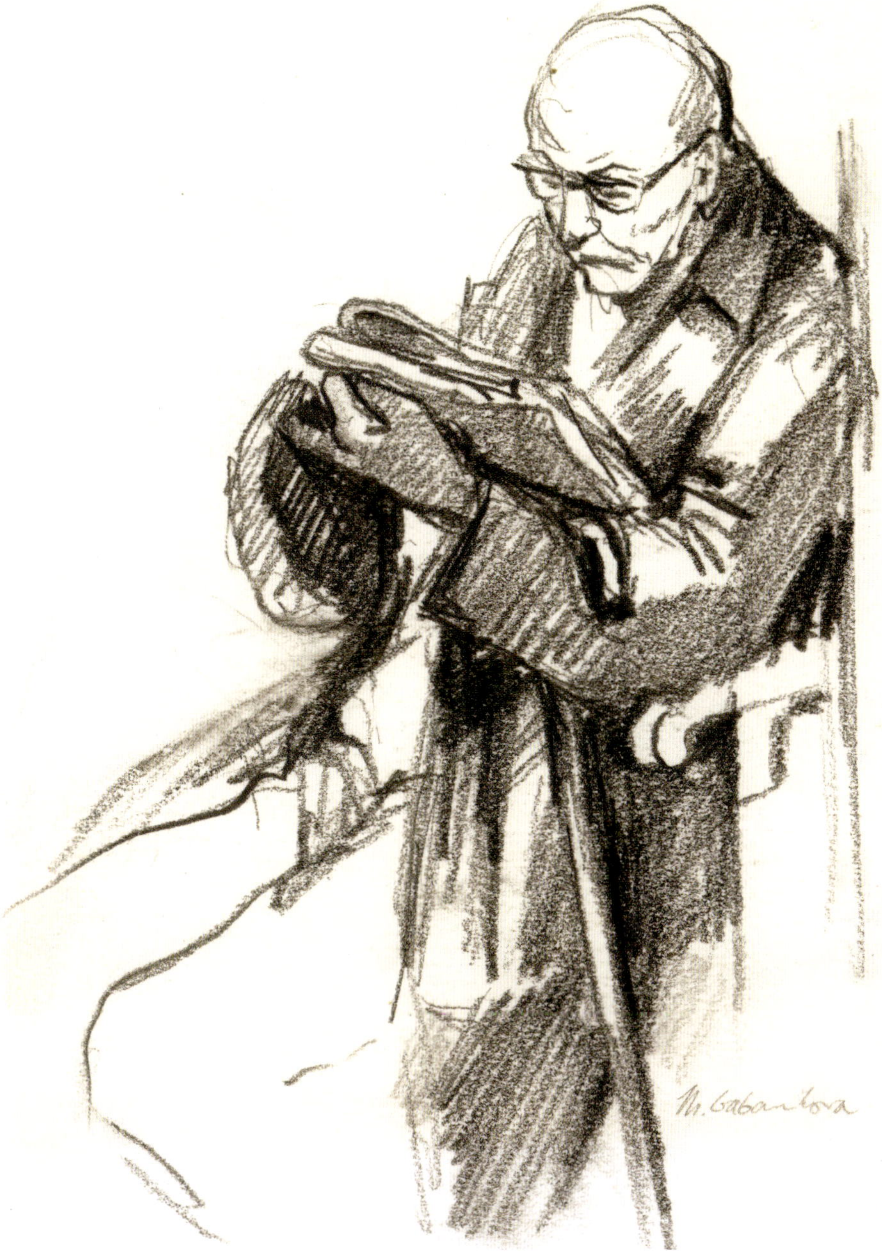

Reader

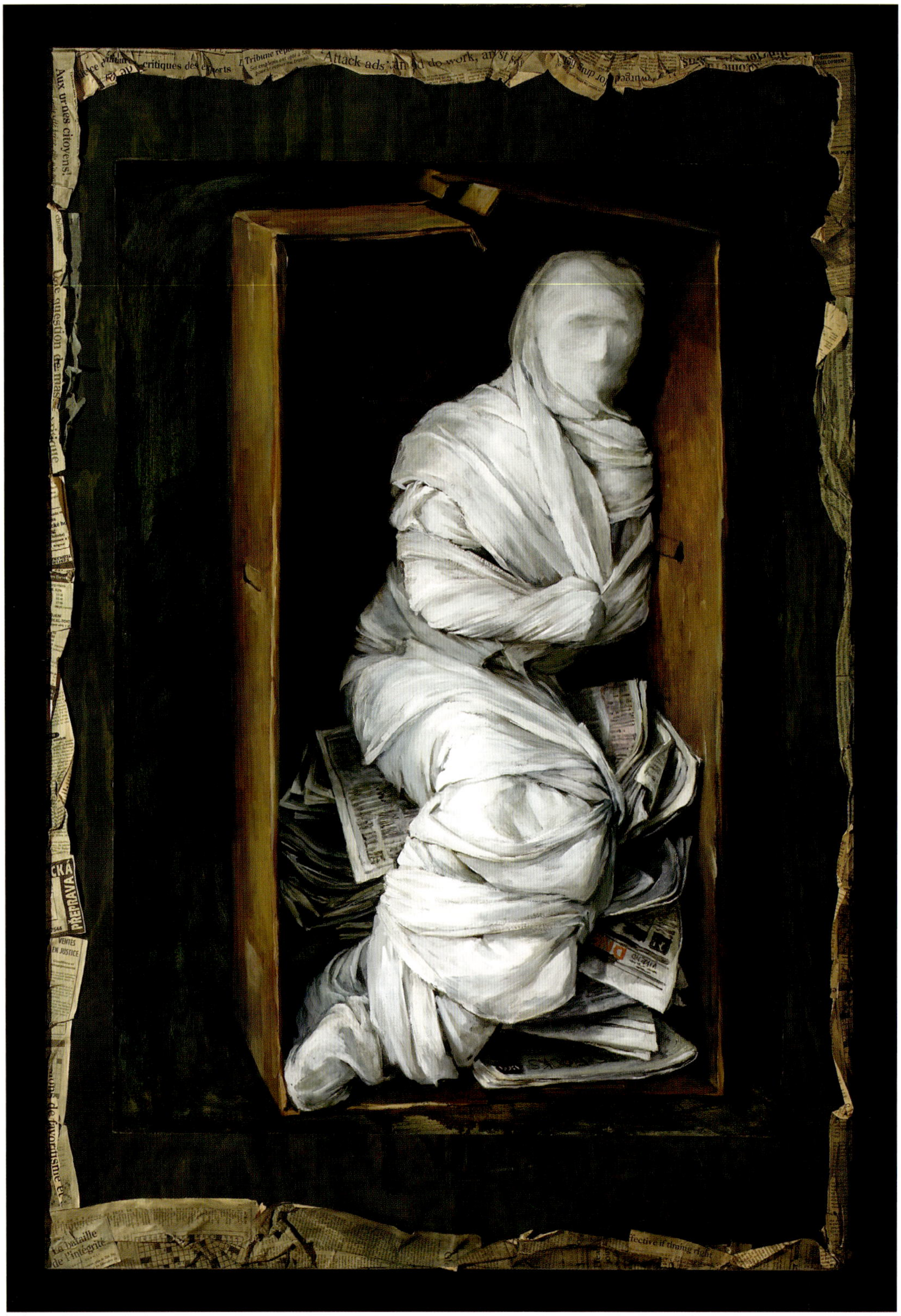

Forgotten News

'*Forgotten News* poignantly shows how quickly "news" of wars, plagues, earthquakes, famines, fires and floods turns old and leaves us indifferent. What's left is a pile of old newspapers turning yellow and brittle. Only a miracle—Lazarus rising from the dead—can still count on some attention.' [Adrienne Dengerink Chaplin, speaking at the opening of the Body Broken exhibition] This painting started as an interpretation of the theme of Lazarus. Later a pile of old newspapers under the mysterious figure in the box added a contemporary element.

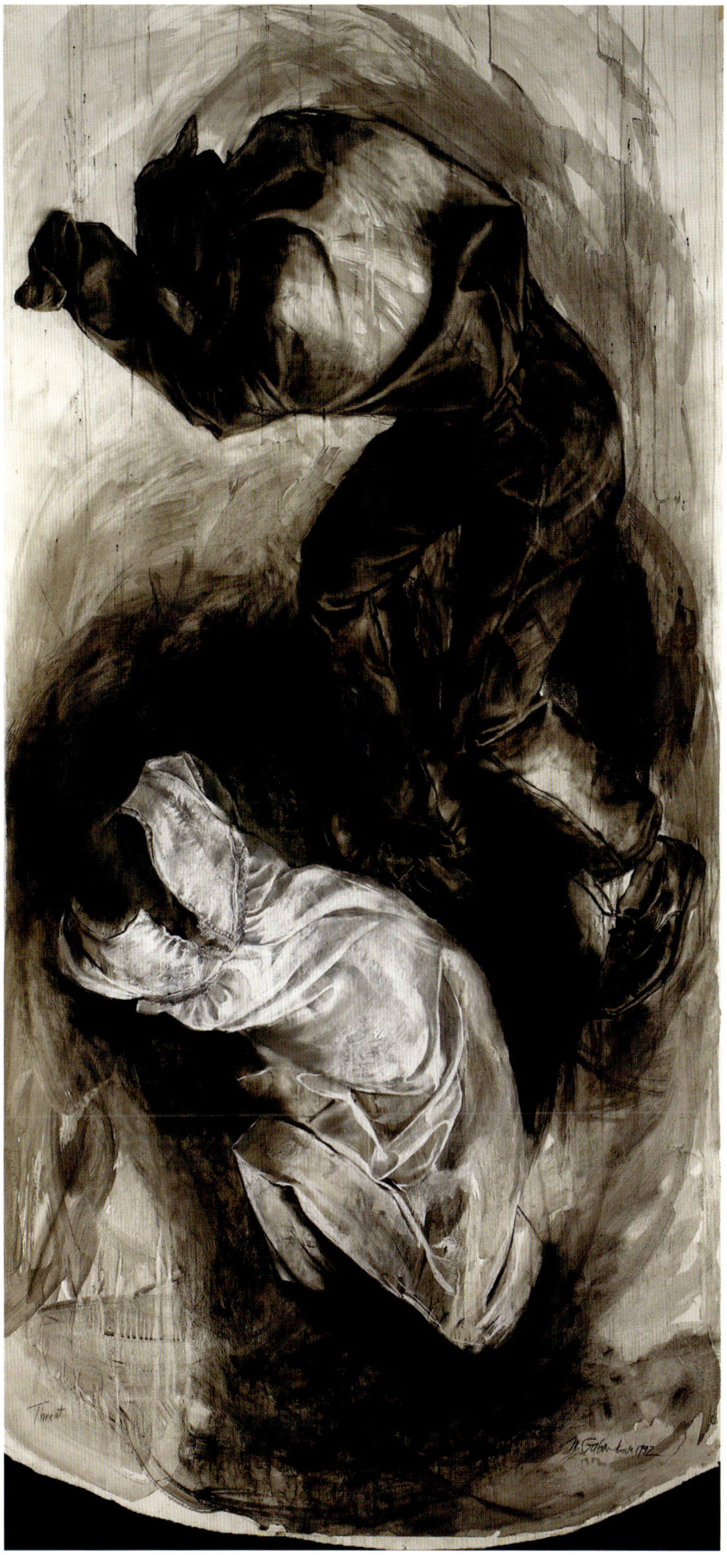

Threat

This large mixed media work is part of a series entitled *Figura Non Grata—The Unwelcome Figure*. The main motif is the idea of absence evoking the reality of presence.

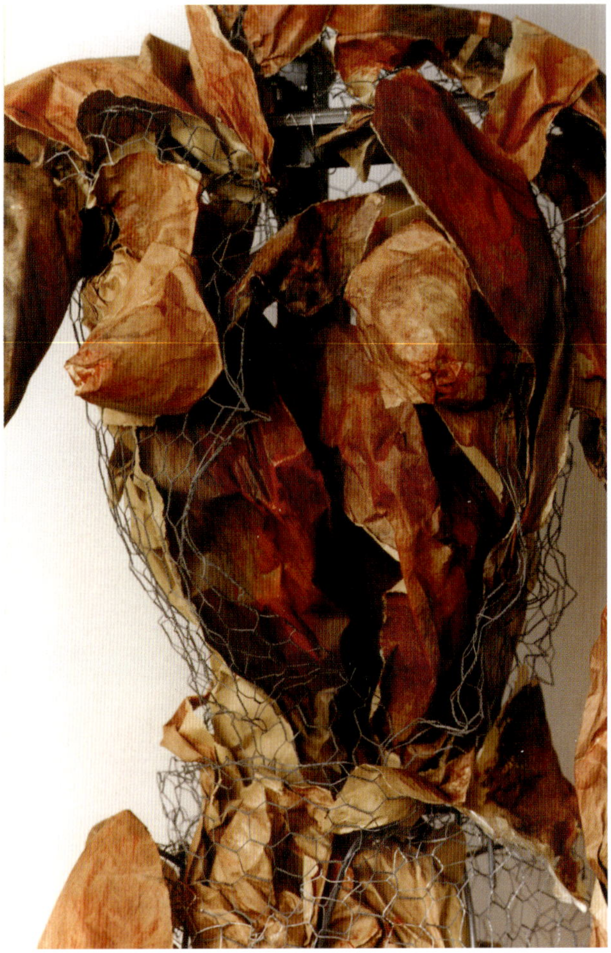

Eve (Sculpture—Installation)

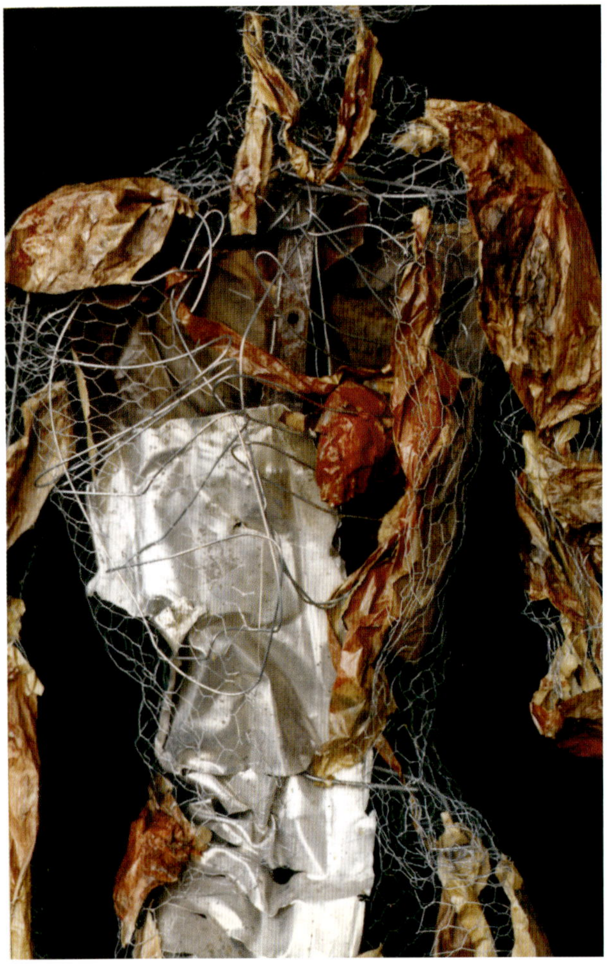

Adam (Sculpture—Installation)

This diptych of Adam and Eve began as two larger-than-life sculptures that I constructed and later painted from. It contemplates how the wonder and poetry of anatomy relate to the temporary nature of beauty, which is devoured by time. The tragic consequences of sin bring on death and decay.

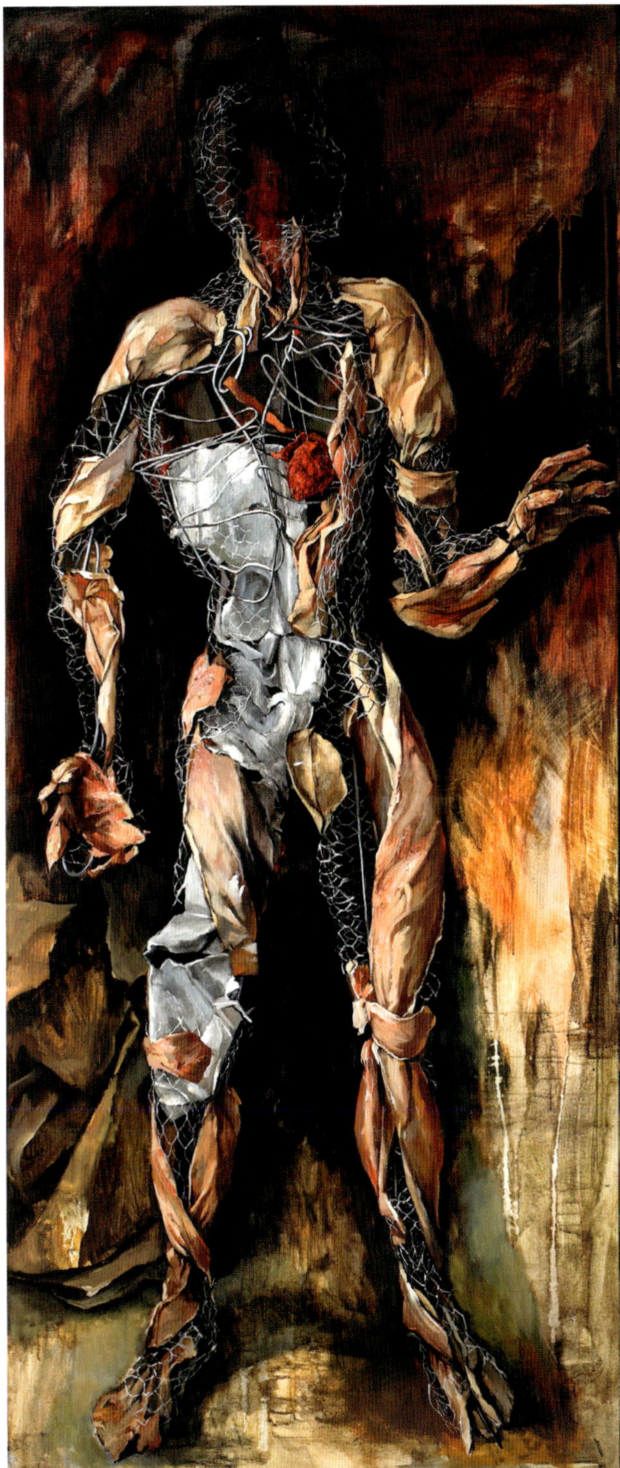

Adam

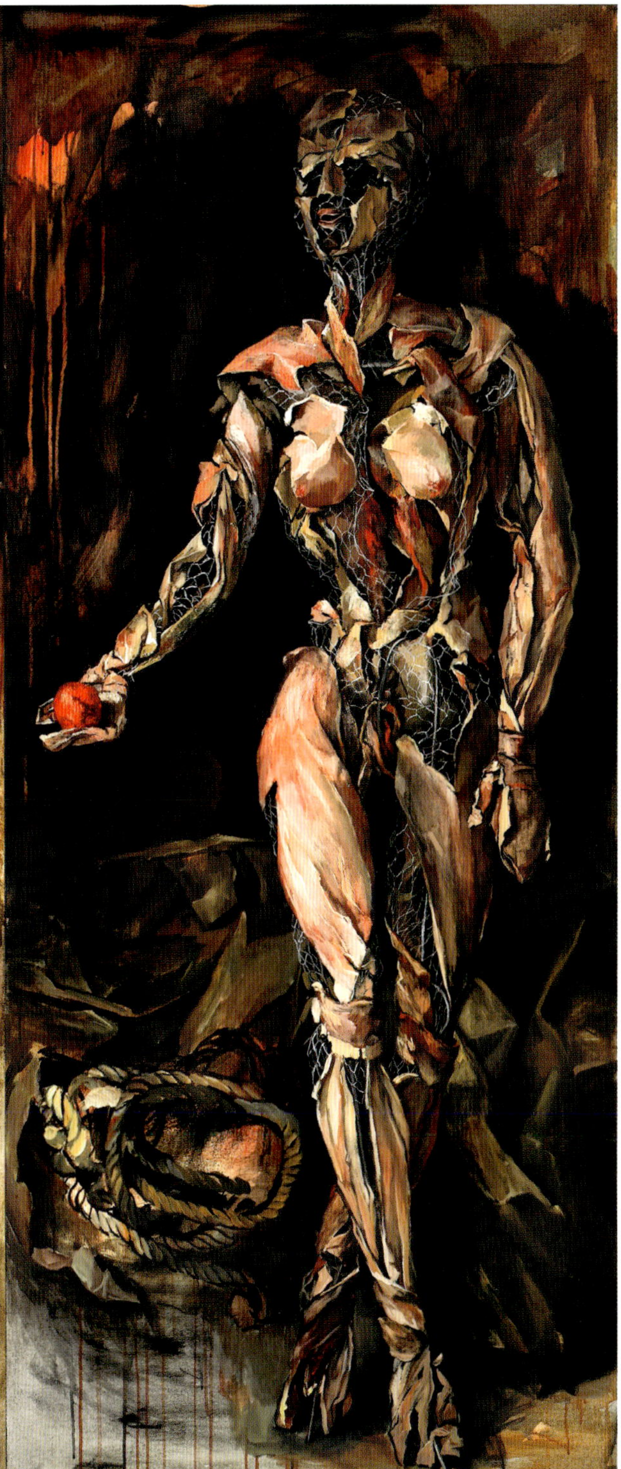

Eve

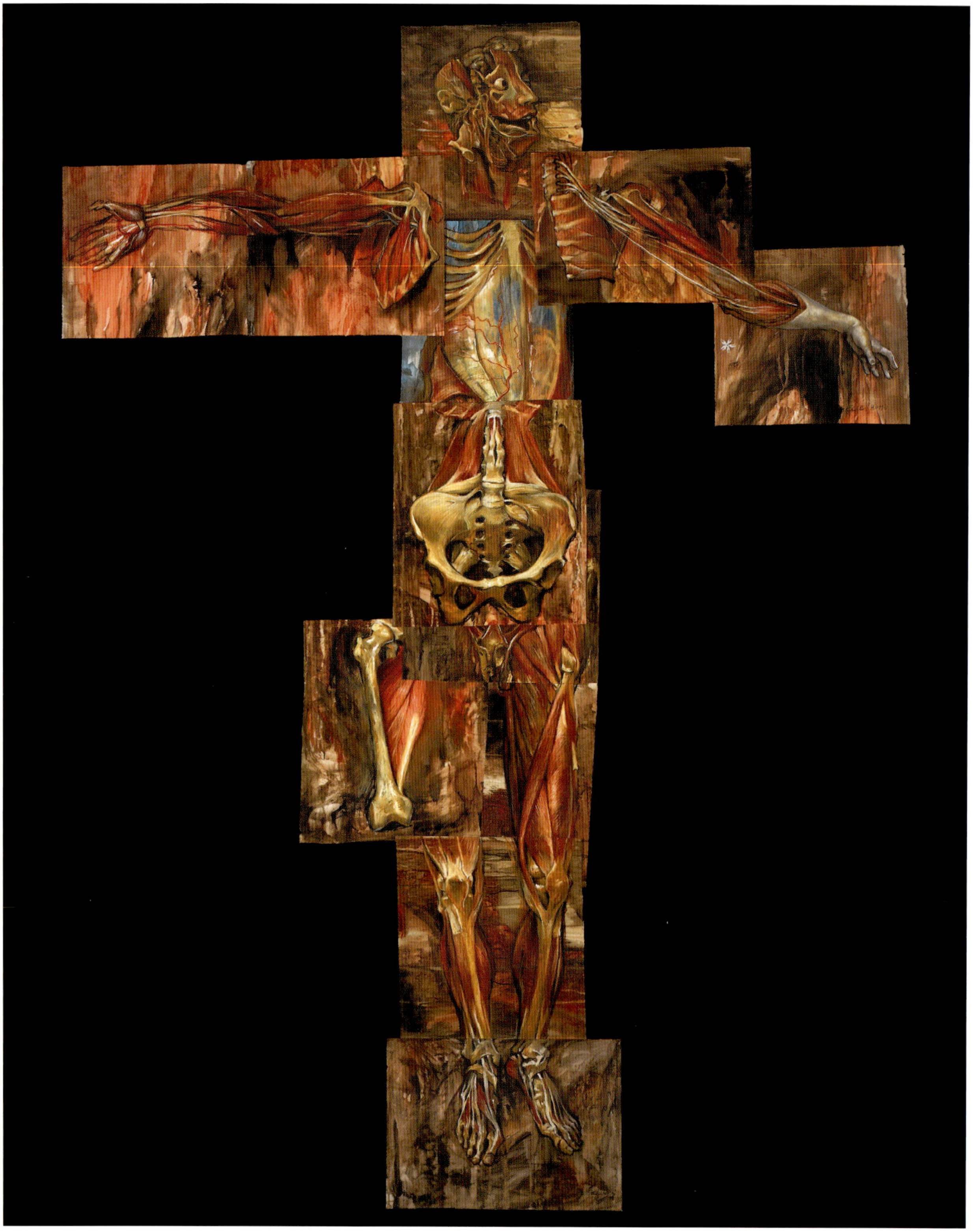

The Cross

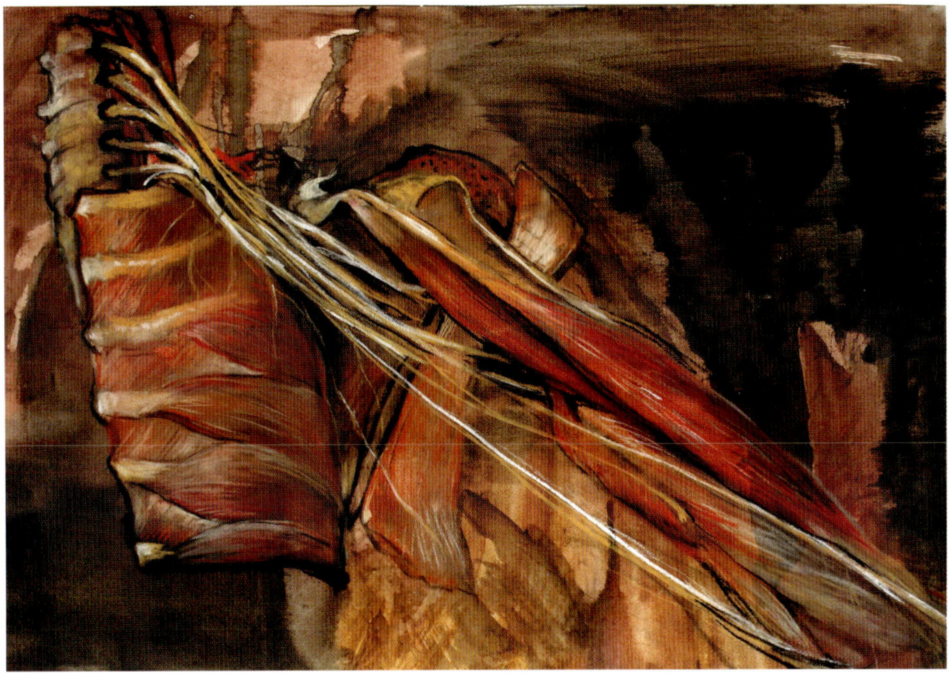

Shoulder

Will you now turn and destroy me?
Remember that you moulded me like clay.
Will you now turn me to dust again?
Did you not pour me out like milk
and curdle me like cheese,
clothe me with skin and flesh
and knit me together with bones and sinews?
You gave me life and showed me kindness,
and in your providence watched over my spirit.
Job 10:8–12

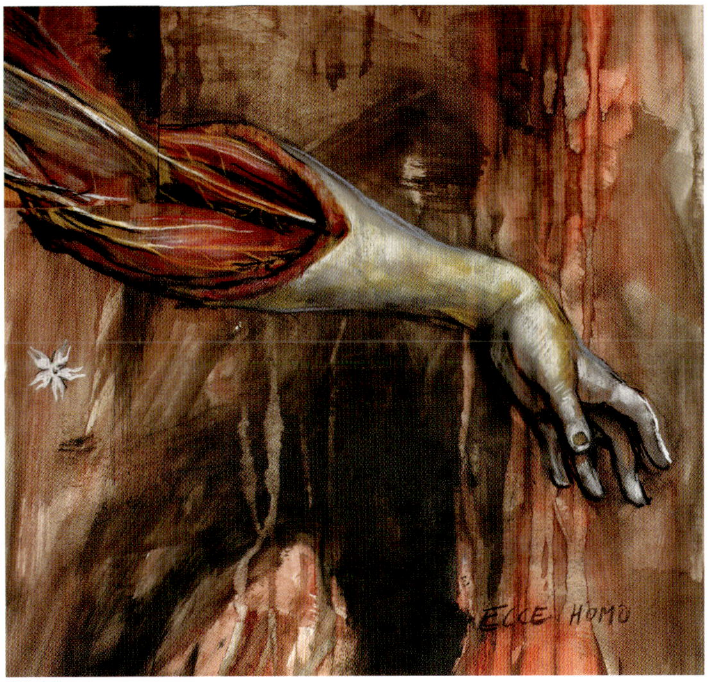

Hand

Assembled in the shape of a cross, these small studies of various parts of the body are based on my work from actual anatomical wax models in the Museo La Specola in Florence, Italy.

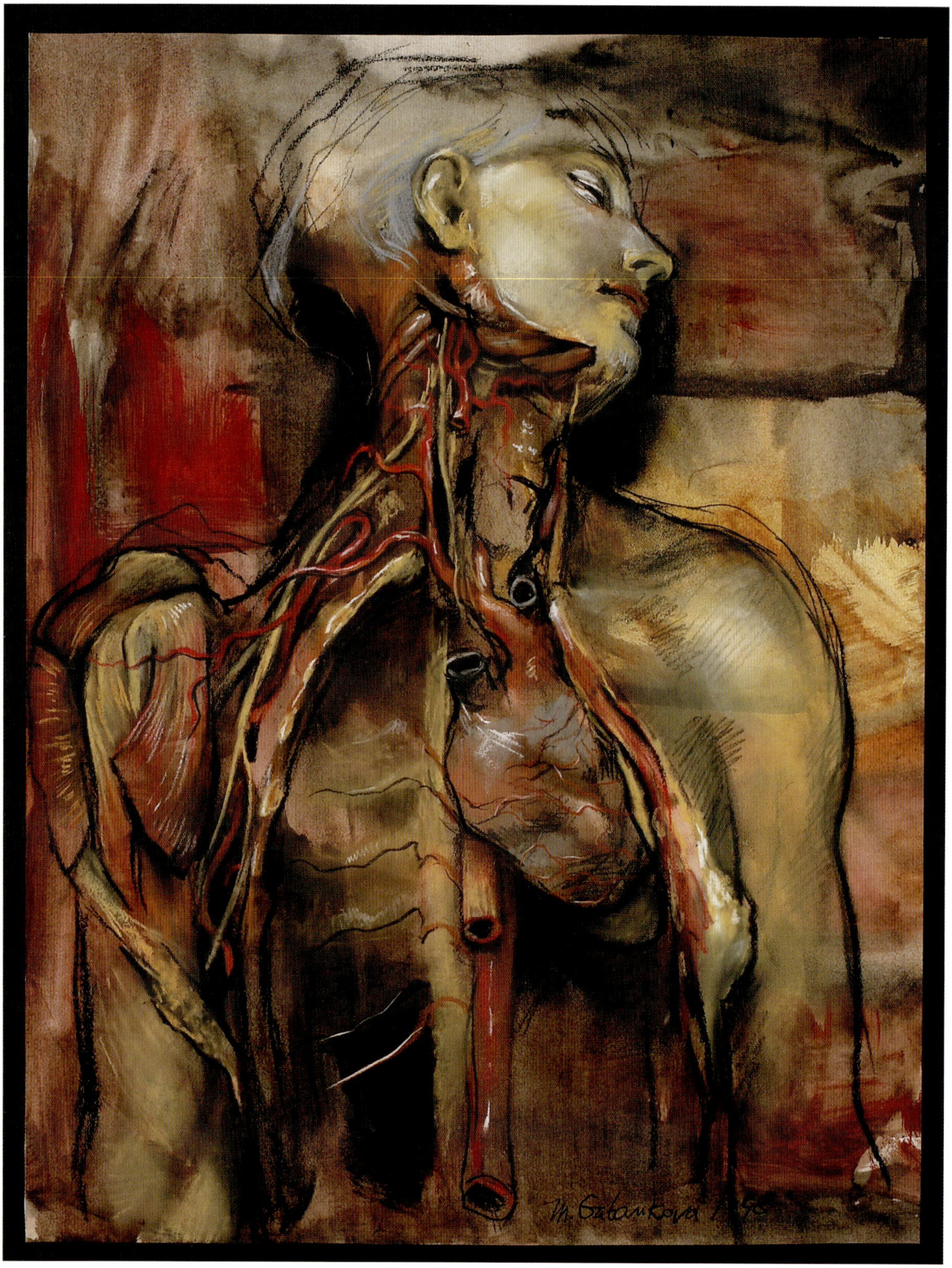

Poetry of the Body

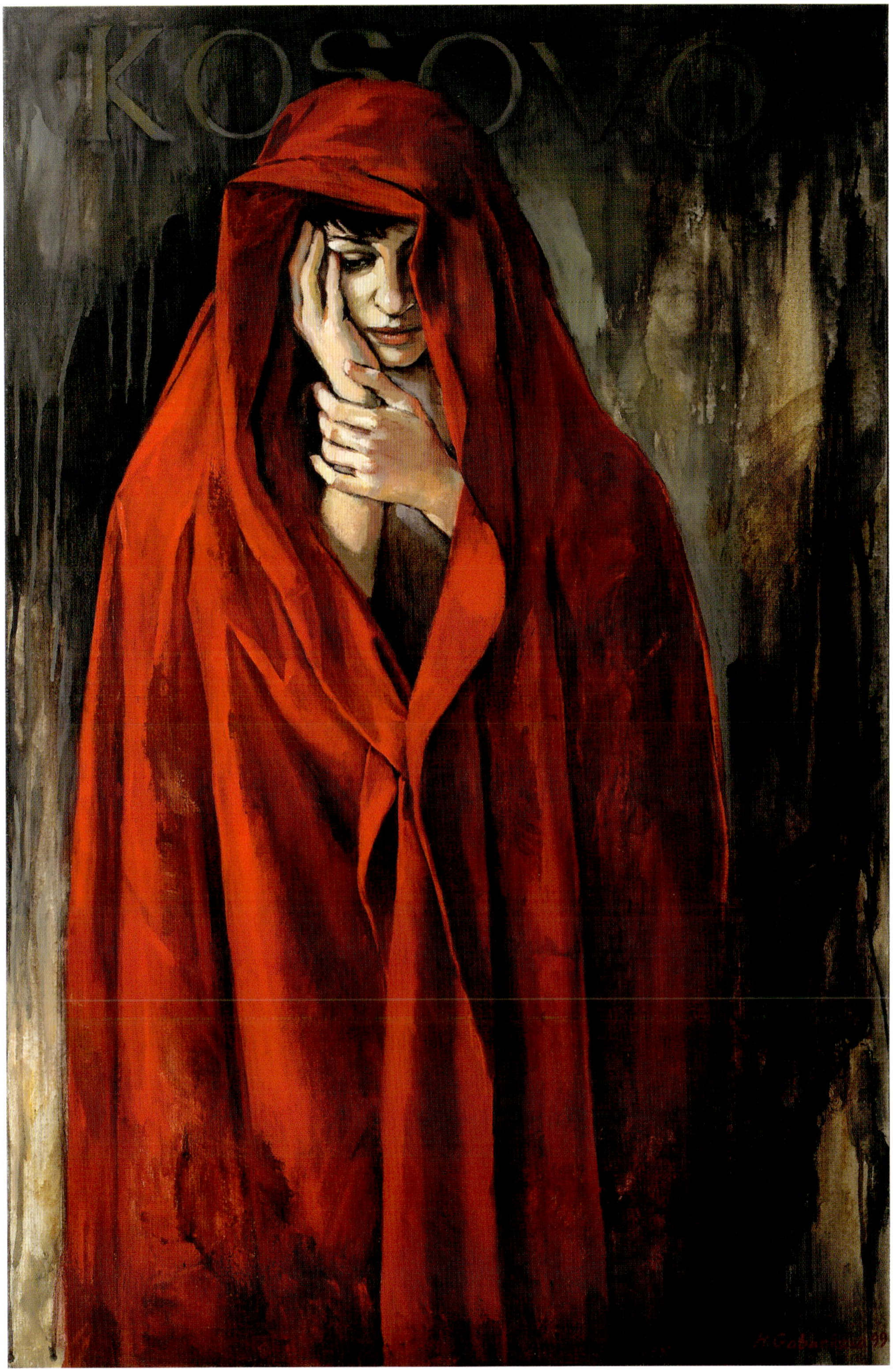

Kosovo

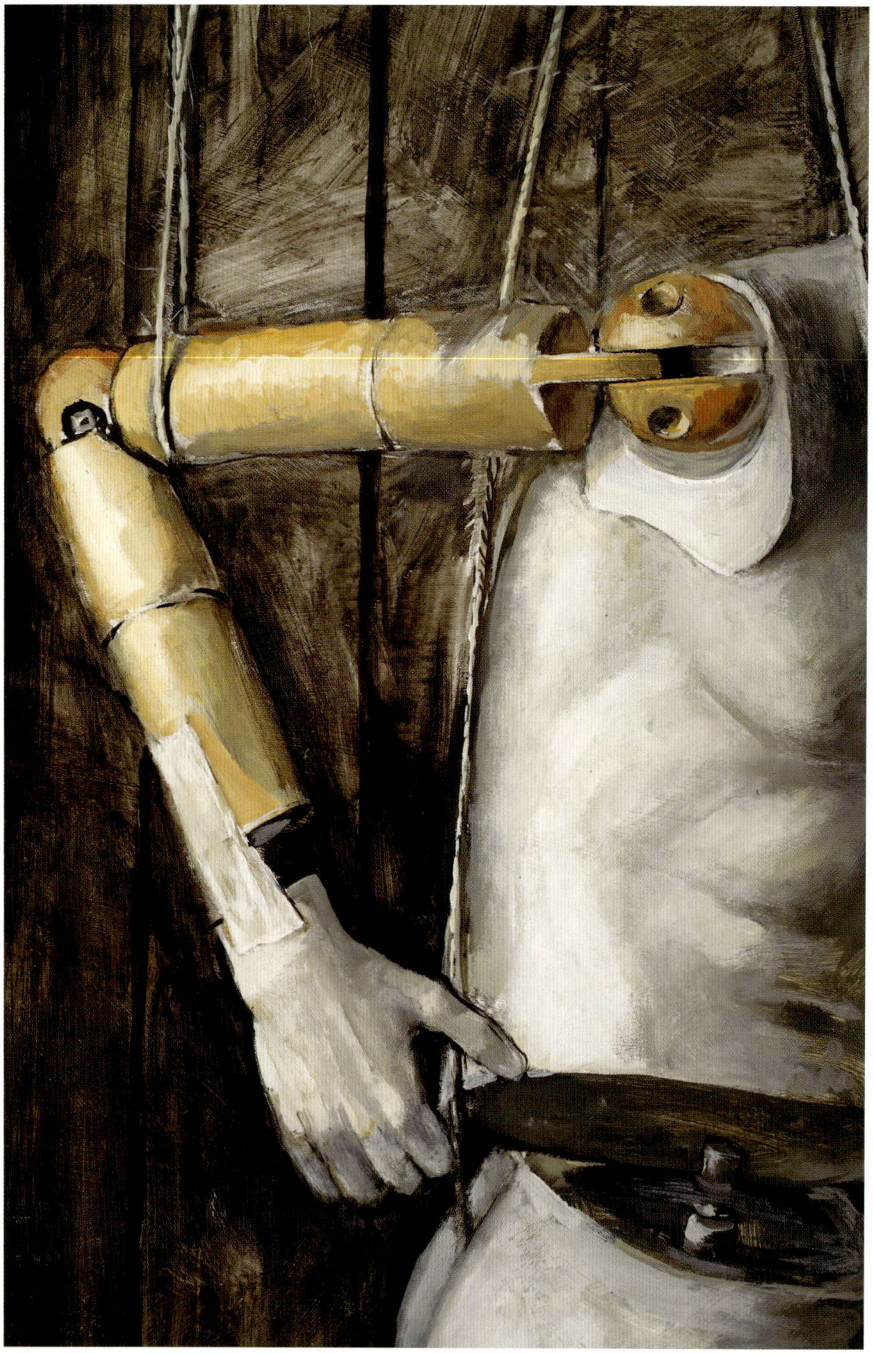
Freedombound (Detail)

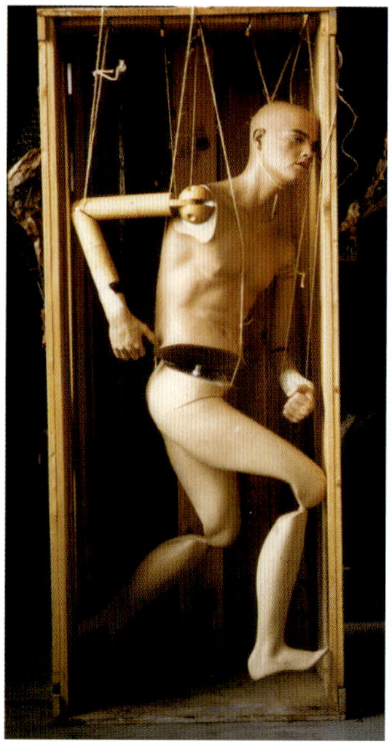
Freedombound (Installation)

In 1992 I began to work with life-size mannequins, using them in various installations as models to paint from. I find the process of transformation from installation to painting a continual source of discovery and fascination. The mannequins serve as intriguing metaphors for the human form and give expression to the often contradictory complexities of our contemporary world. My intent was to explore how through our brokenness God can awaken in us a longing for him.

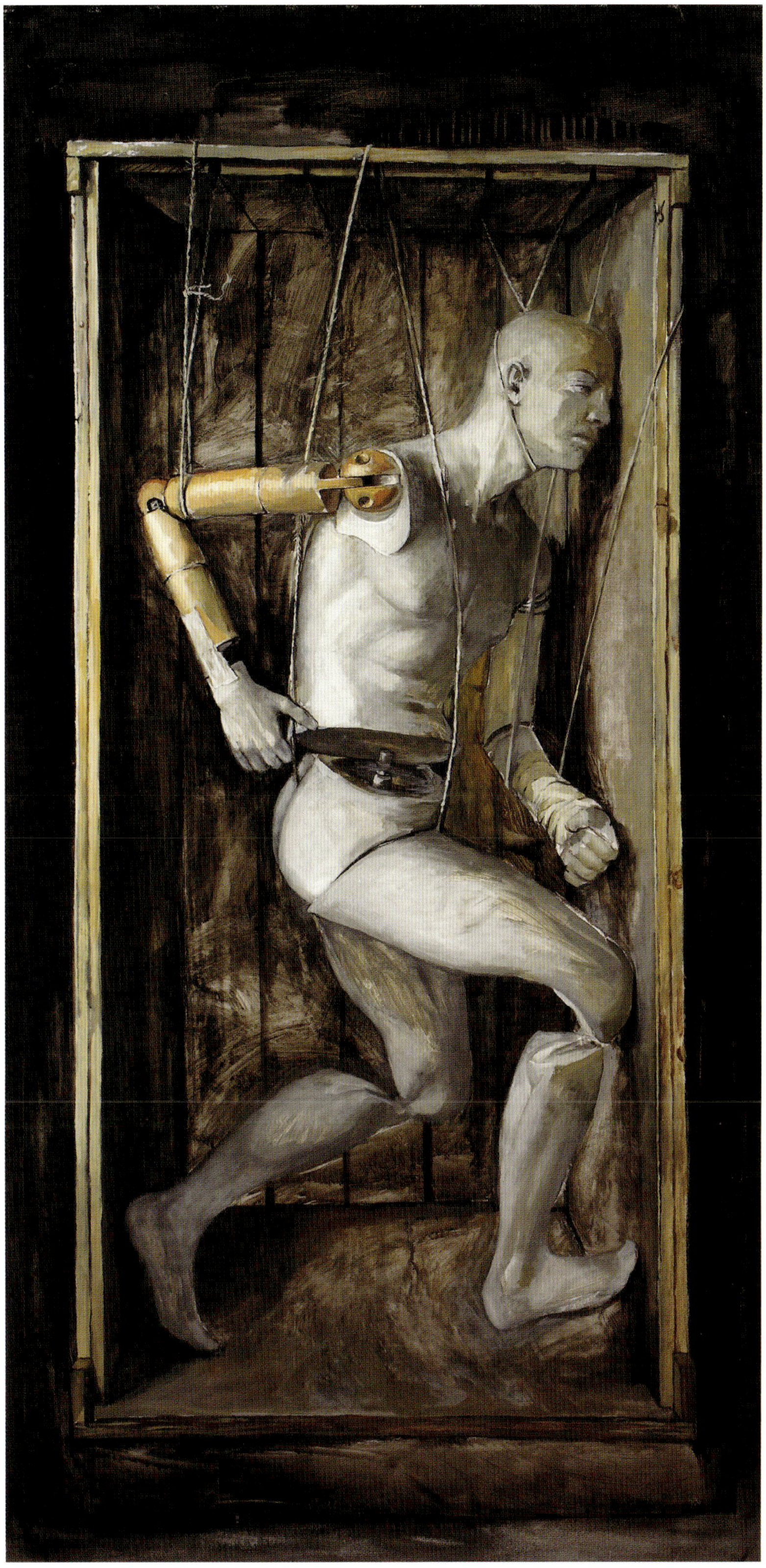

Freedombound

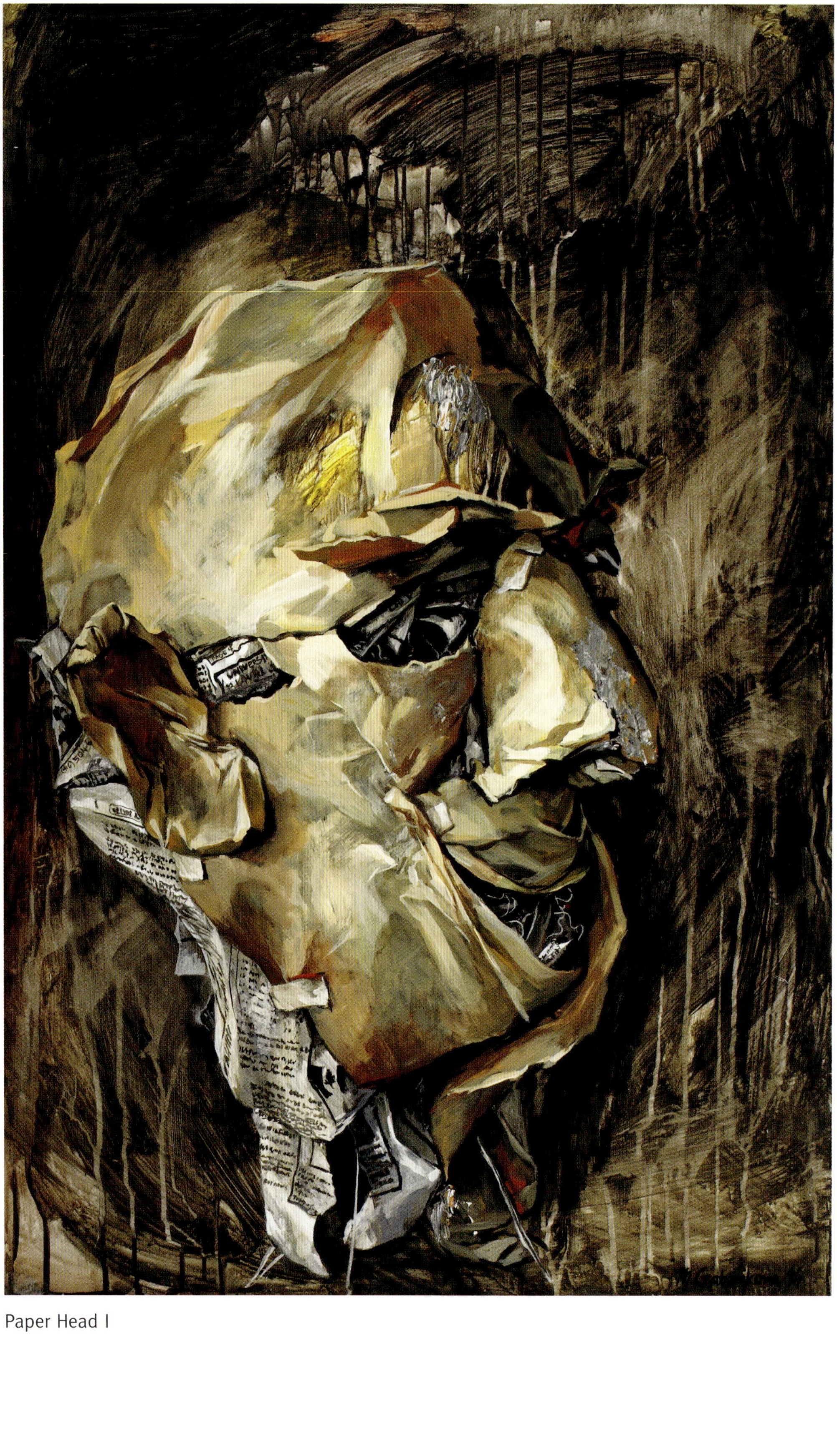

Paper Head I

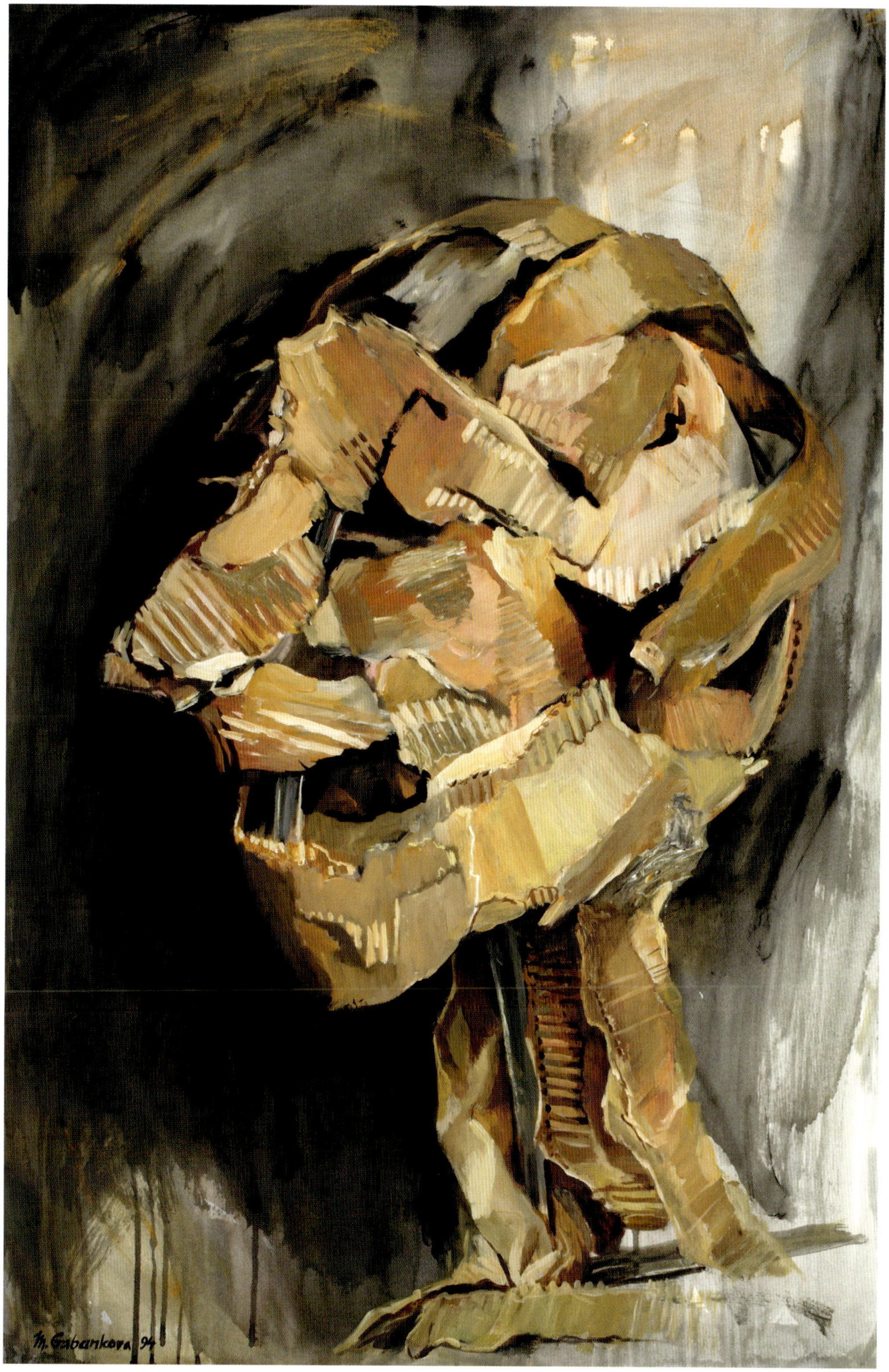

Paper Head II

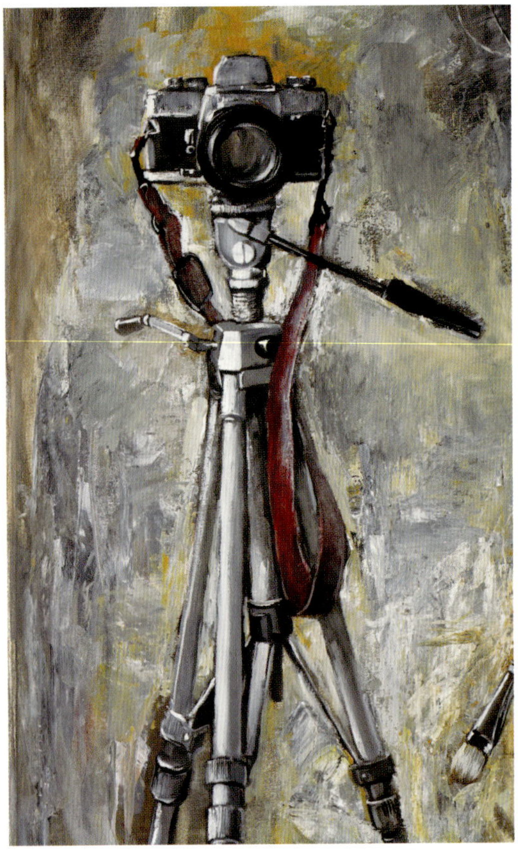

The Joker's New Clothes (Detail 1)

This image is about truth-telling, on the edge between laughter and a scream. It is a self-portrait in part—part mannequin becoming human—part human on the way to becoming a puppet. The painting alludes to Hans Christian Andersen's fairy tale The Emperor's New Clothes. The awkwardness of the ill-fitted body parts combined with the playful pose suggests the tension of my struggle for meaning and faith in God amidst the incongruous complexities—both joyful and disturbing—of our present world.

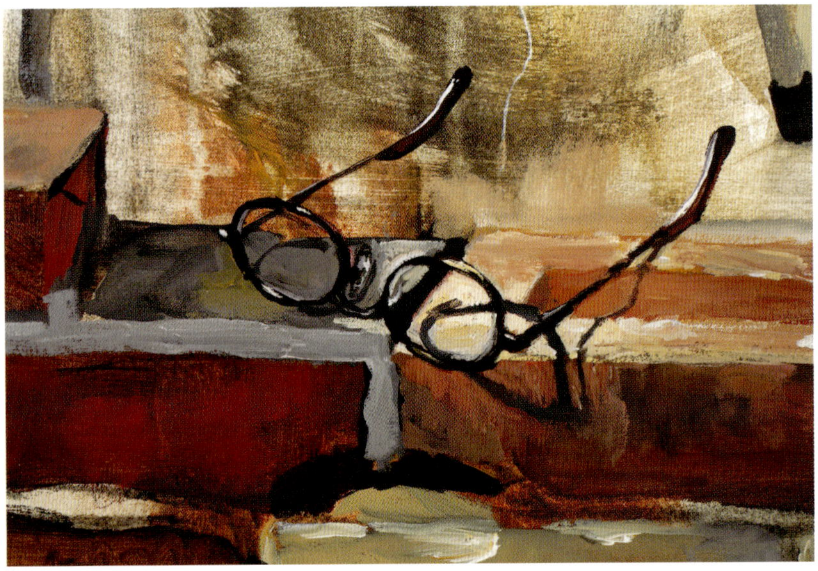

The Joker's New Clothes (Detail 2)

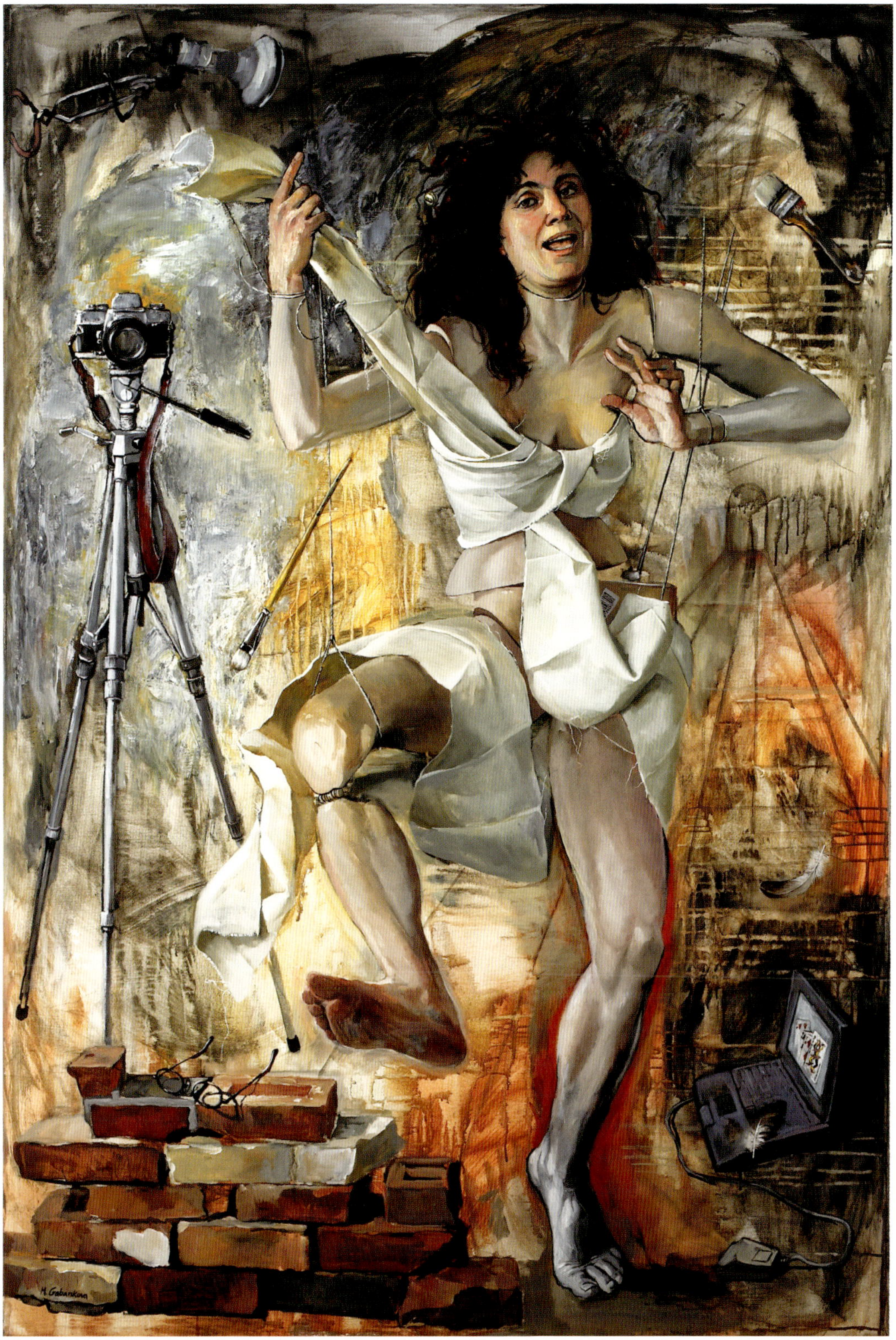

The Joker's New Clothes

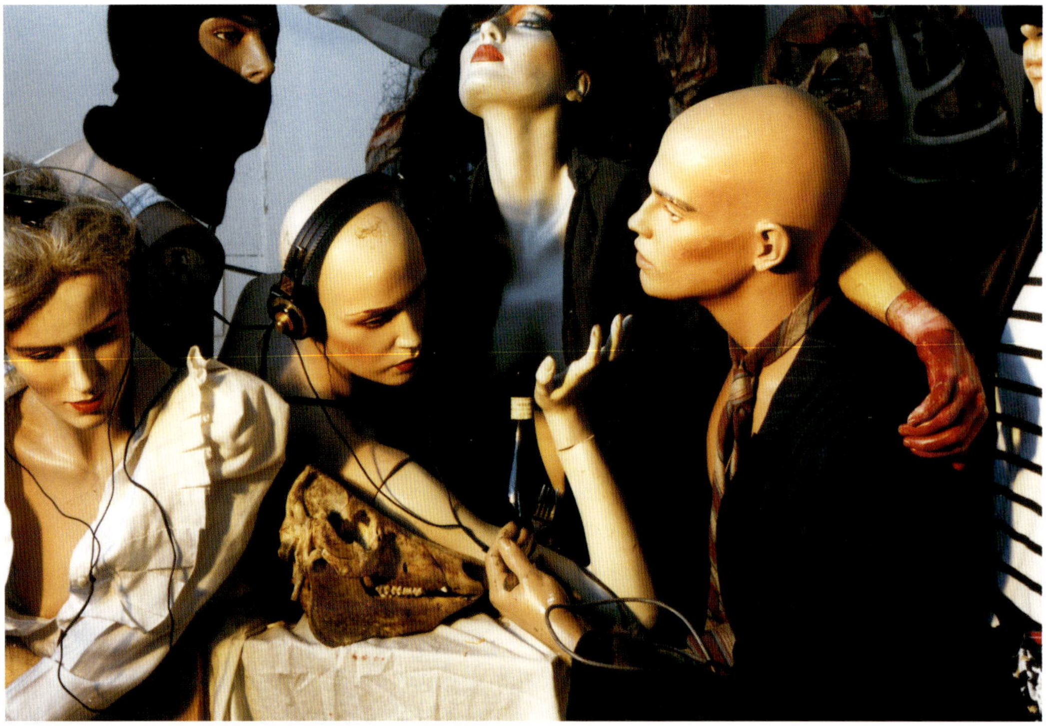

Report from a Leaky Boat (Installation)

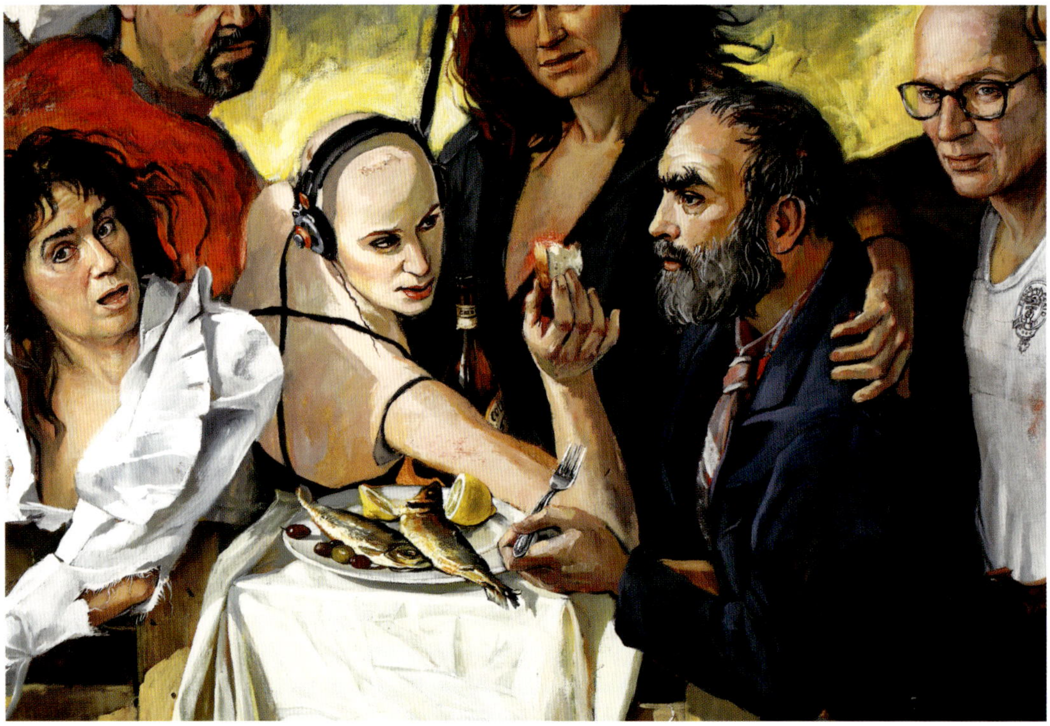

Report from a Leaky Boat (Detail)

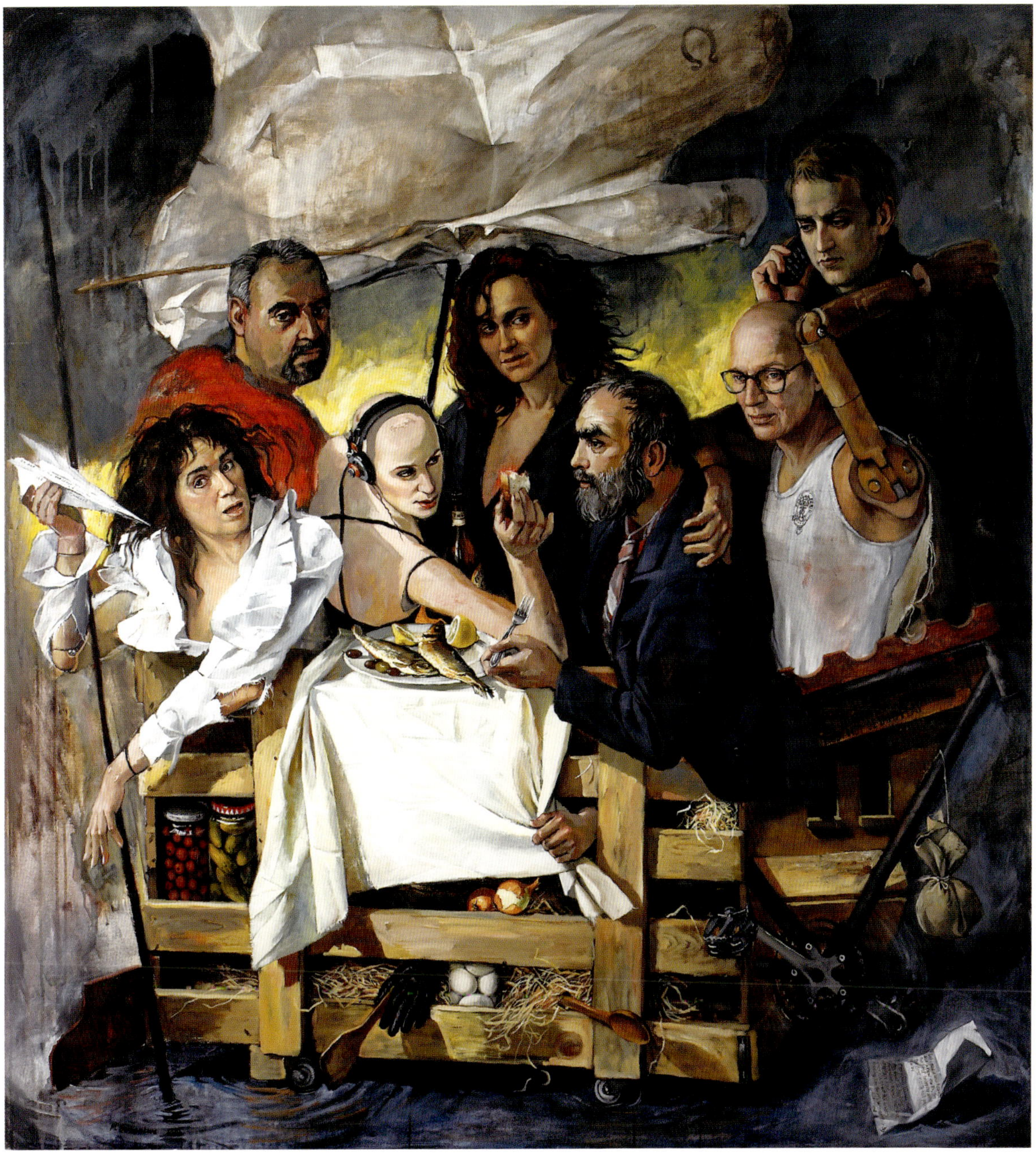

Report from a Leaky Boat

A small painting by Hieronymus Bosch titled *The Ship of Fools* was loosely connected to the development of this painting, which is an allegory of the journey through life. At its core is a questioning and examining of my own life and the lives of my close friends and of the direction of our journey. The title is partly derived from an apocalyptic song by Leonard Cohen, 'Everybody Knows' where 'Everybody knows that the boat is leaking.' The other source is a quotation from the book of Revelation: 'And I saw a new heaven and a new earth' (Rev 21:1). These words are written on a piece of paper floating on the water in the lower-right corner. I am reflecting on my faith and about 'work(ing) out (my) salvation with fear and trembling' (Phil 2:12). The boat in this painting is a symbolic reference, as are the alpha and omega on the sail, the first and the last letters of Greek alphabet ('I am the Alpha and the Omega, the beginning and the end, says the Lord', Rev 22:13).

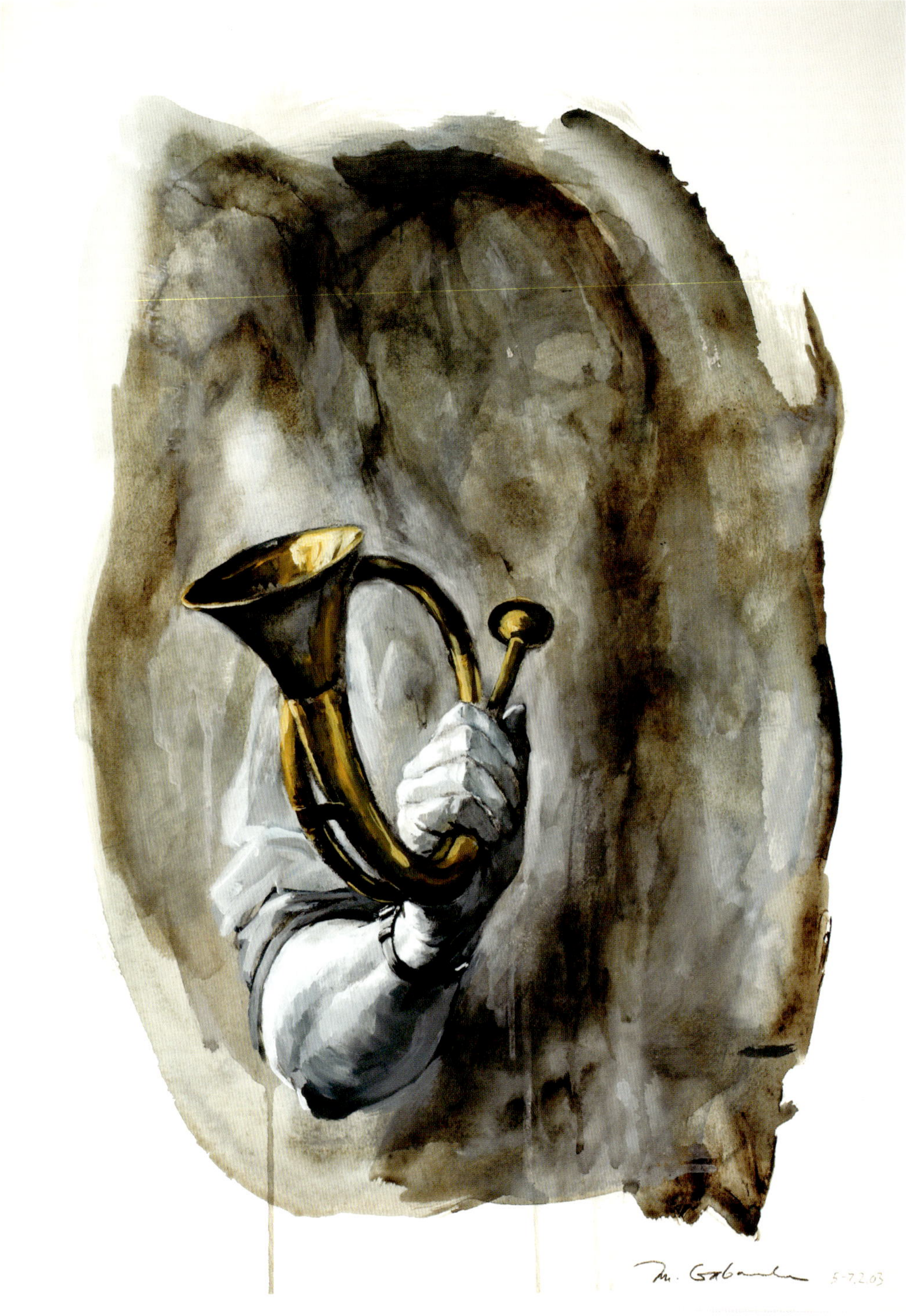

Messenger—Hand I

These are studies for the larger 'Messengers' compositions on themes from the book of Revelation. I enjoyed bringing the more defined forms of the hands out of the loose chaotic acrylic washes.

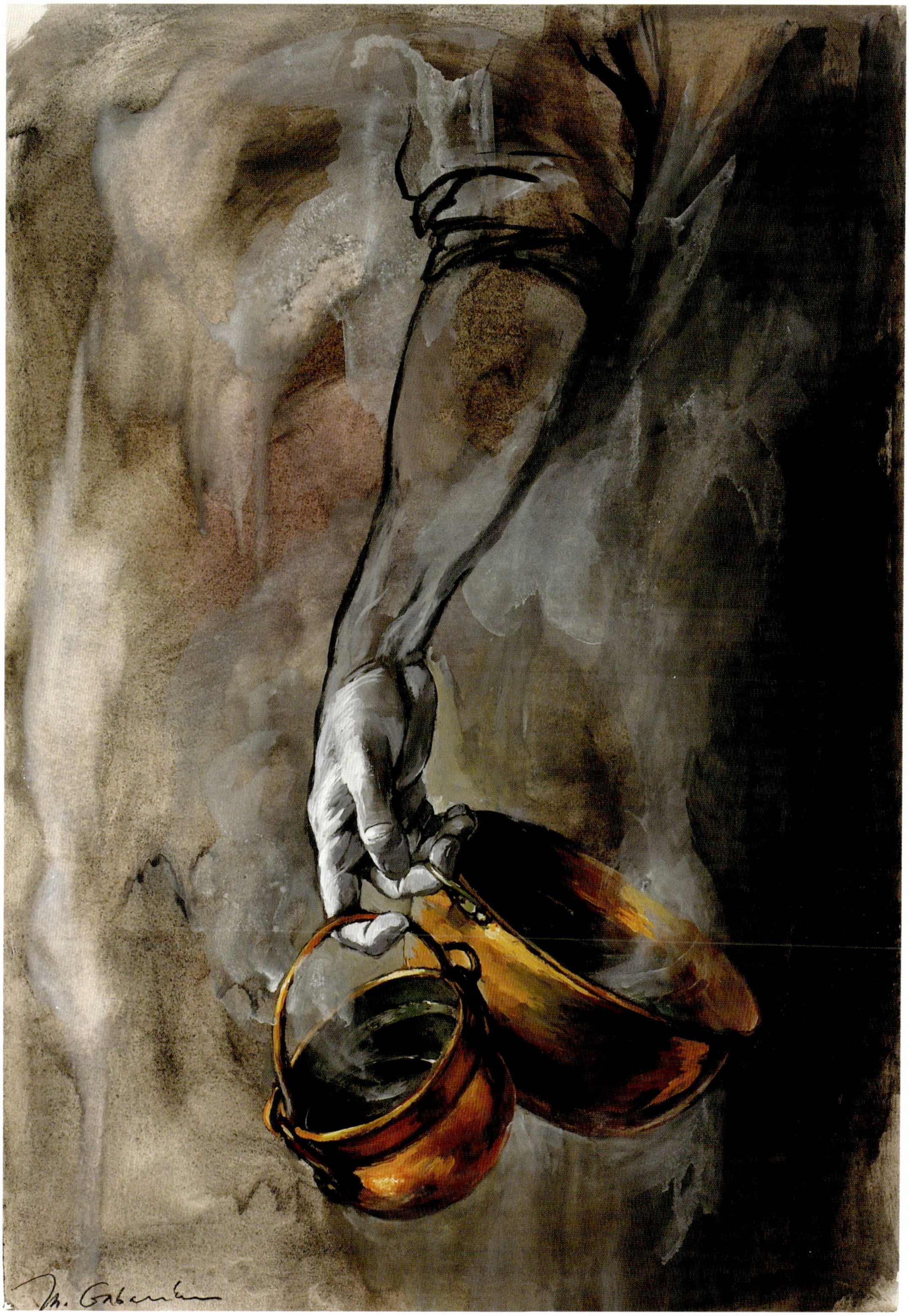

Messenger—Hand II

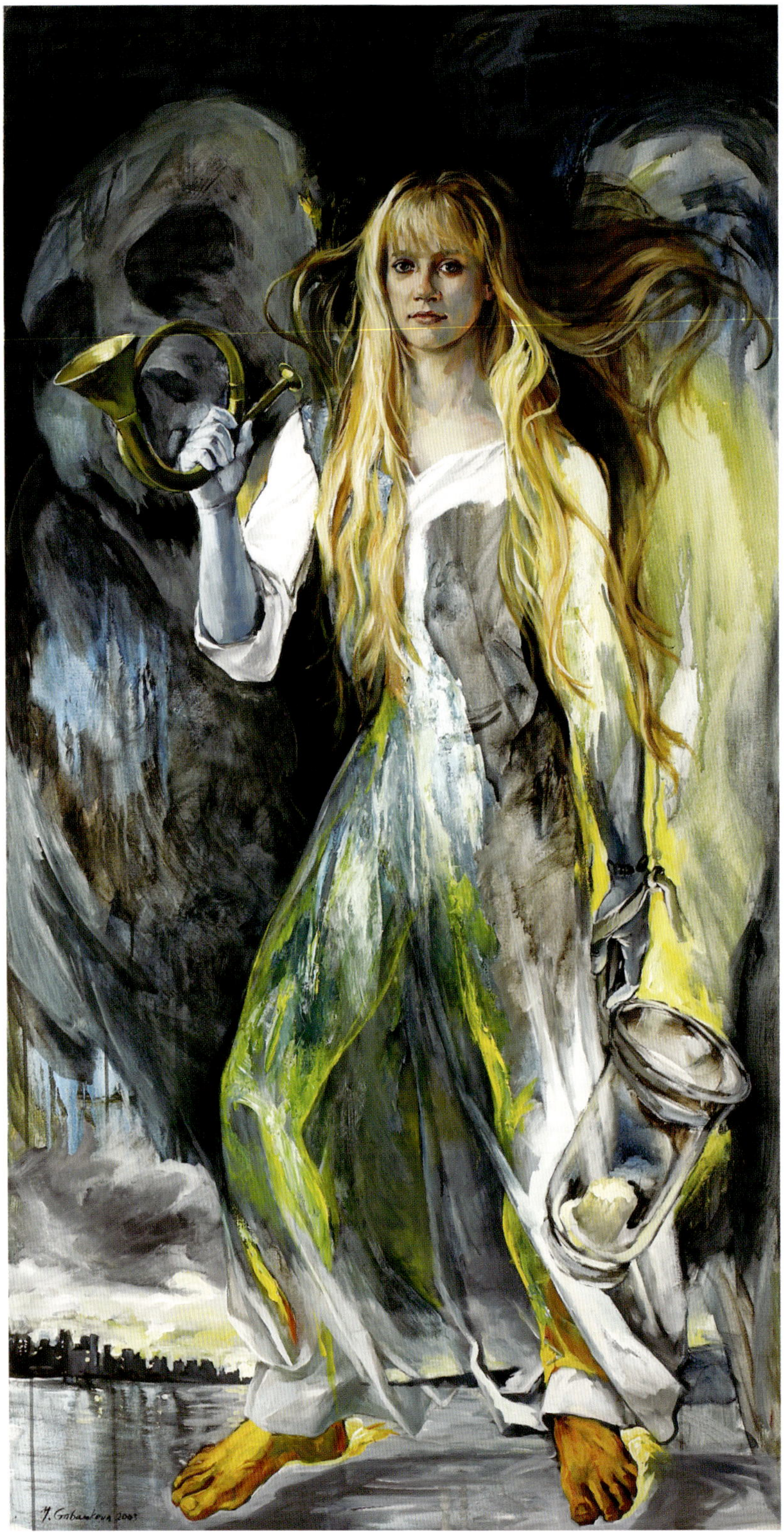

Messenger I

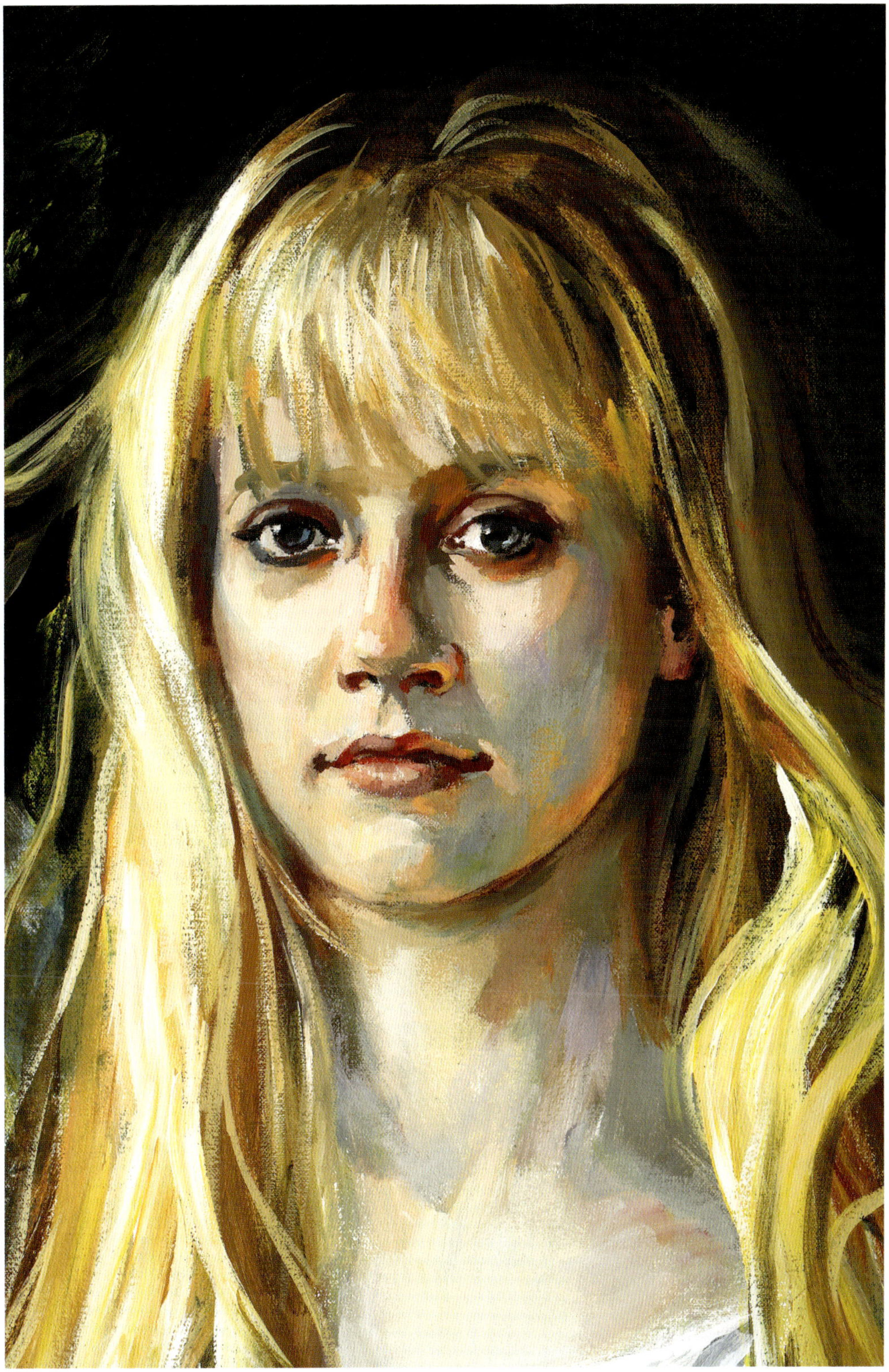

Messenger I (Detail)

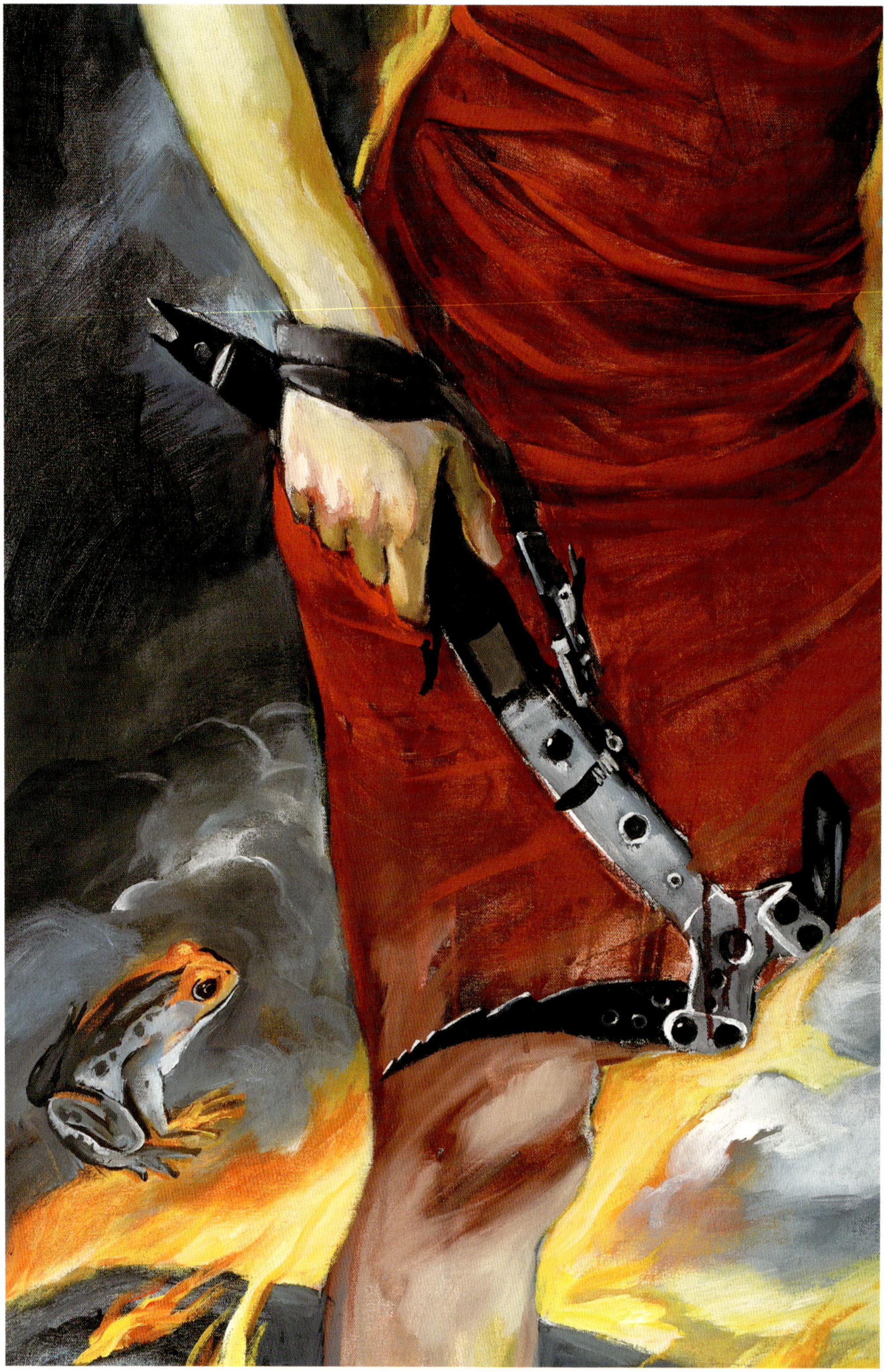
Messenger II (Detail)

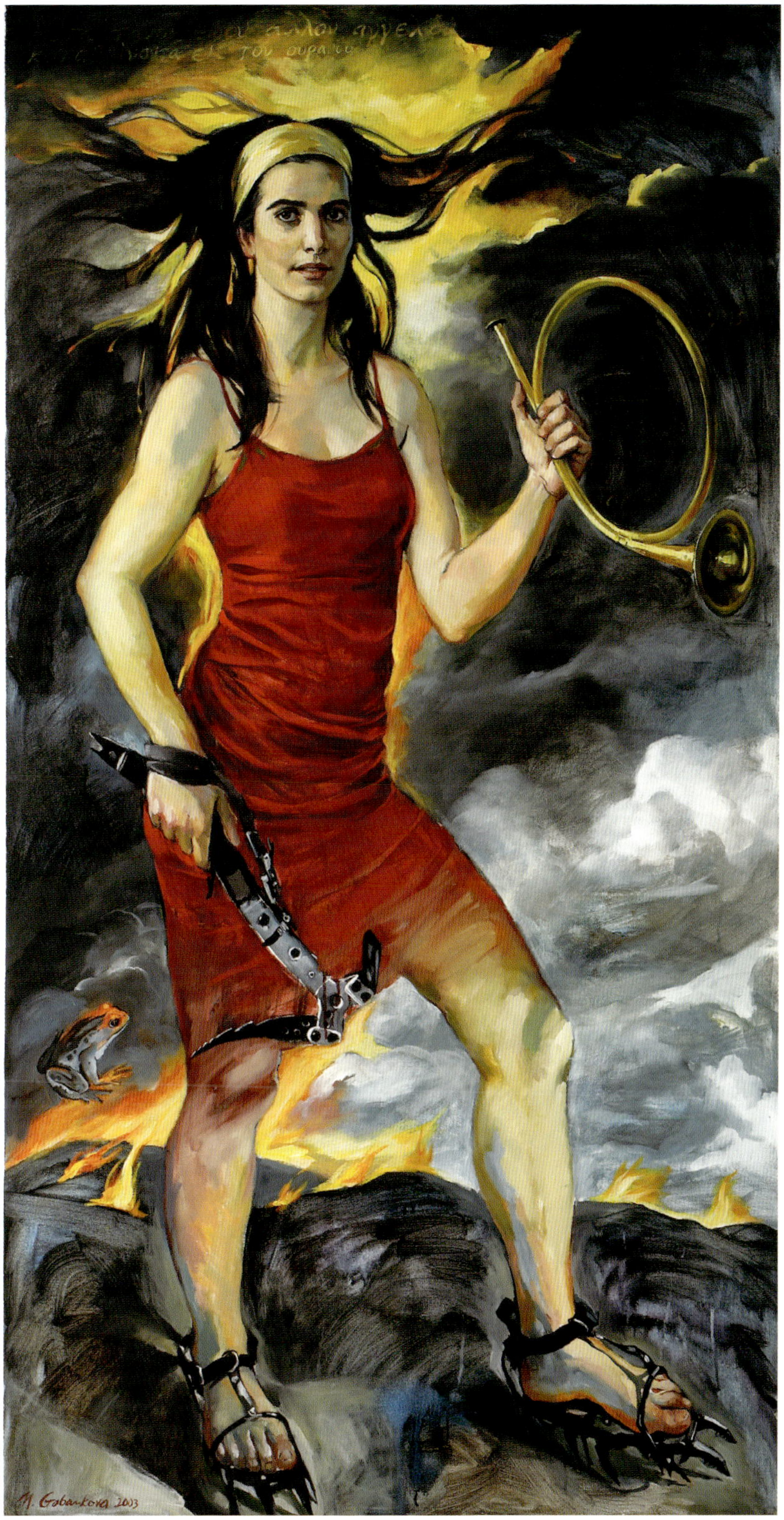

Messenger II

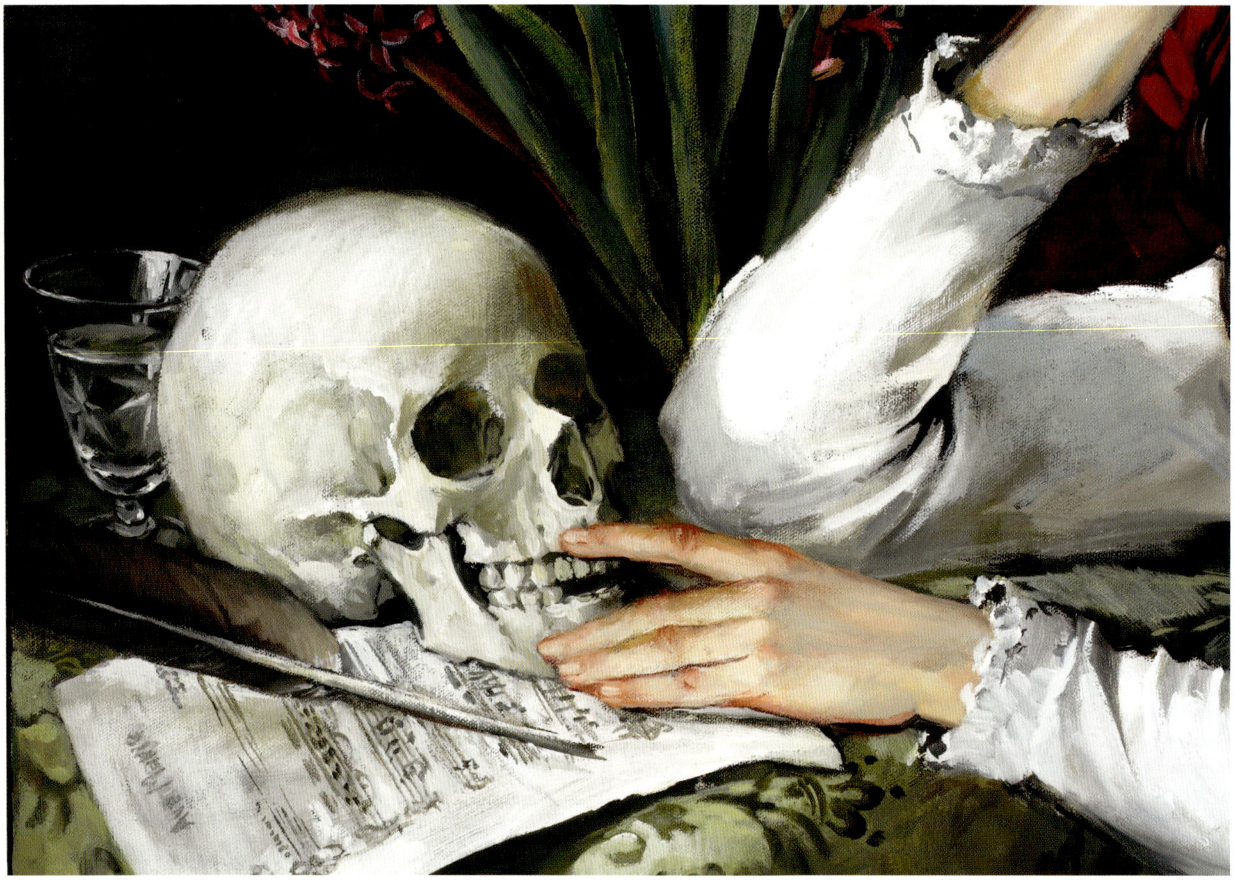

Melancholia (Hand detail)

This painting began with the idea of a nude seated with a skull—a contemporary Mary Magdalene. Then I overpainted the initial stage and added the colourful draperies, books, the hyacinth and musical instruments. I began to think of the composition as a Christian allegory and associated it with Albrecht Dürer's engraving *Melencolia*, where a winged figure represents an artistic genius despairing of inspiration. The hyacinth in my painting is a symbol of Christian prudence, peace of mind and a desire for heaven; the triangle, represents the Trinity. Several of the colours used also have symbolic meaning. Black, the symbol of death and the underworld in general, suggests mourning, sickness, negation and death; black and white together, however, symbolize humility and purity of life; red, the colour of blood, is associated with the emotions of both love and hate; yellow may either be an emblem of the sun and divinity, or it may suggest infernal light, degradation, jealousy, treason and deceit; white represents innocence of soul, purity and holiness of life. (See George Ferguson, *Signs & Symbols in Christian Art*, Oxford University Press).

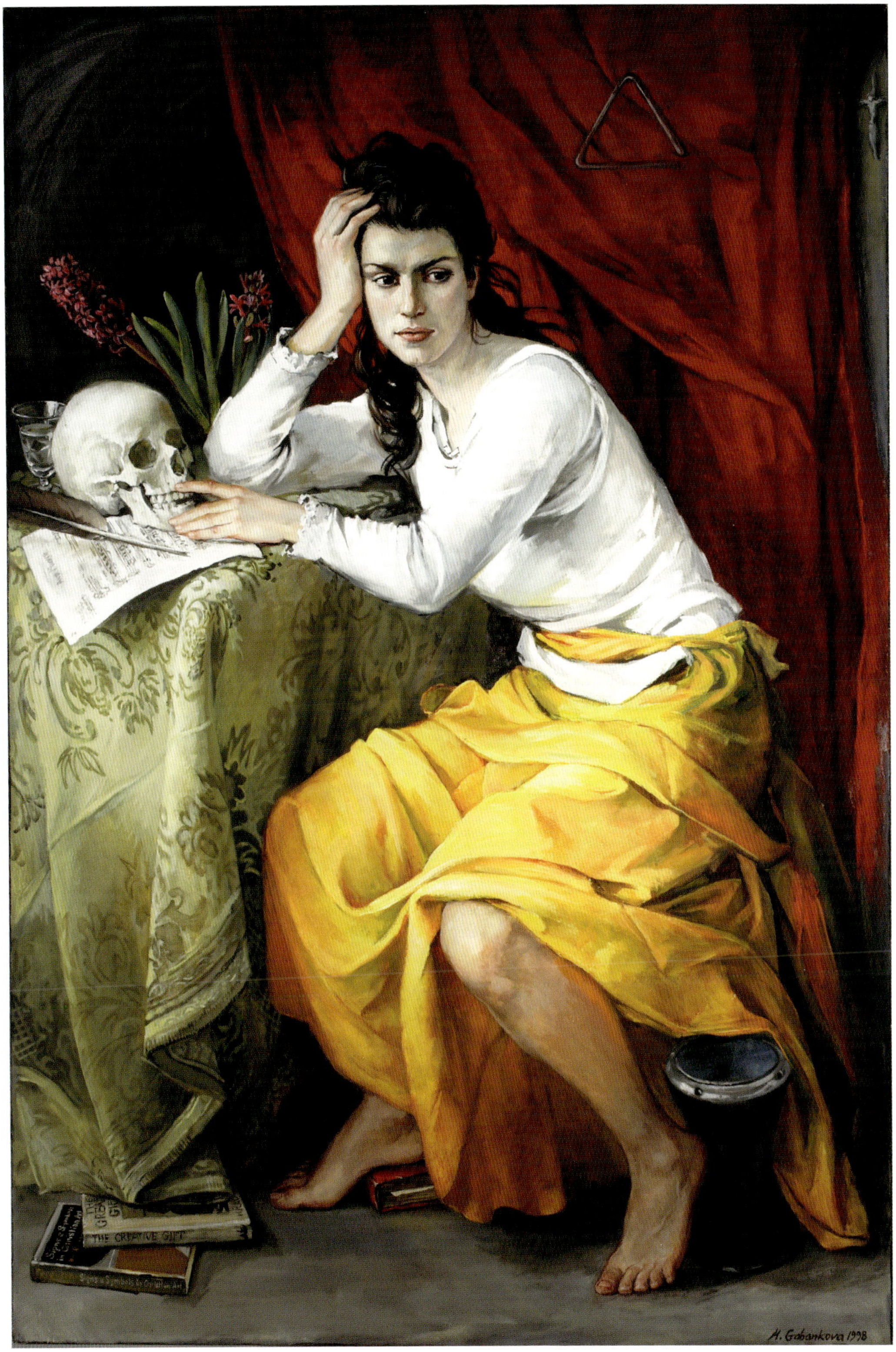

Melancholia

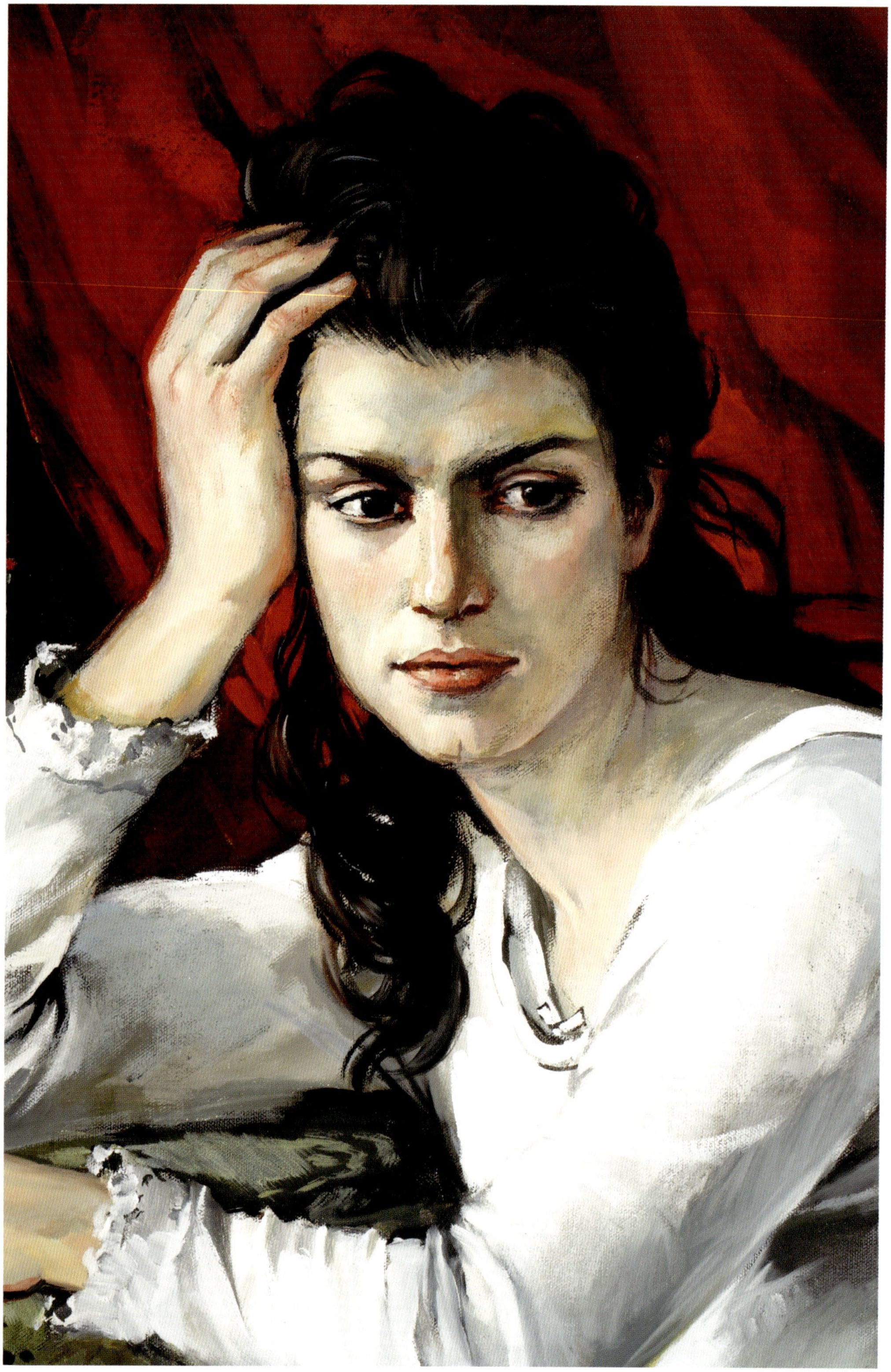

Melancholia (Detail)

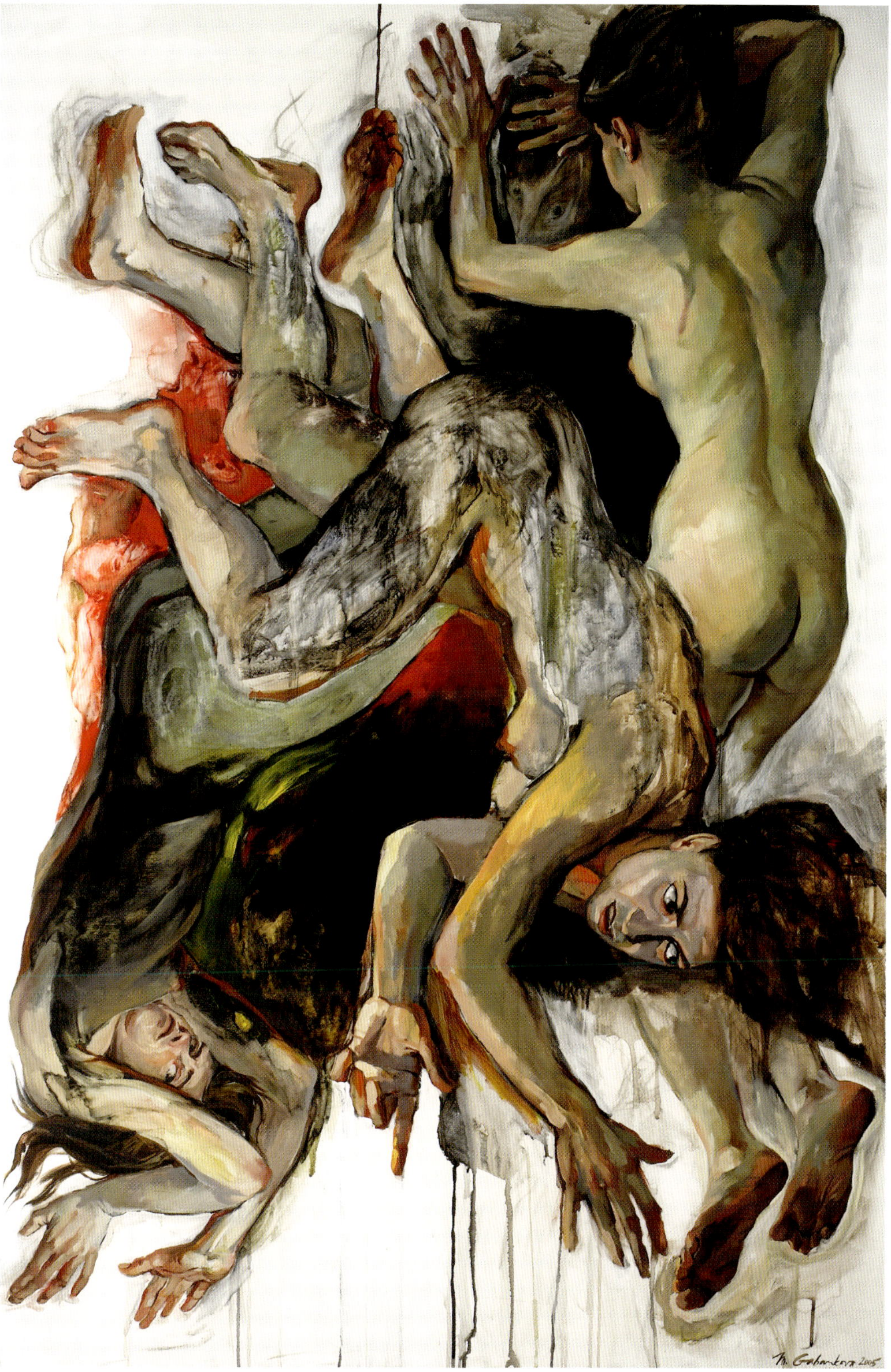

The Fall

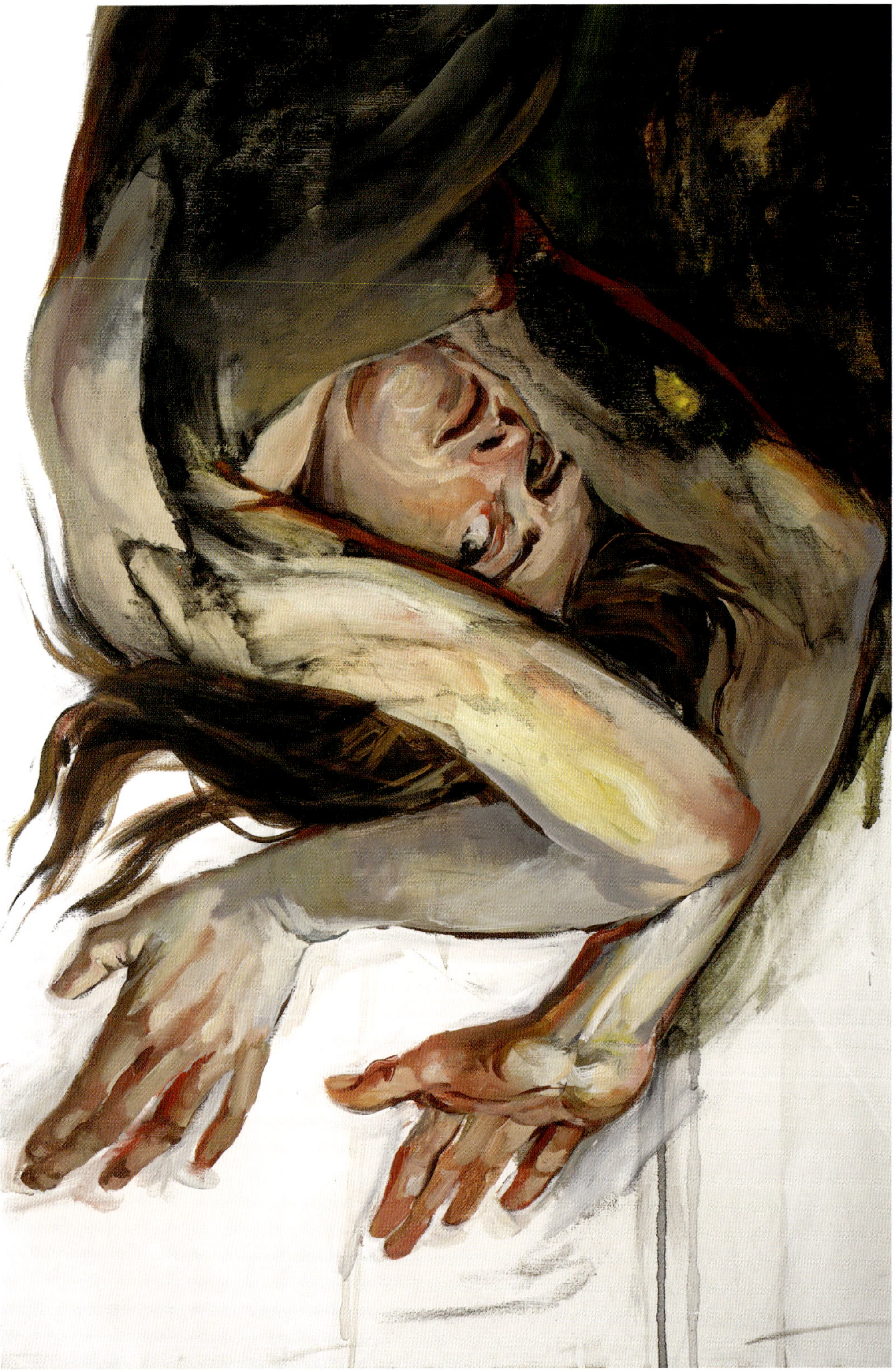

The Fall (Detail 1)

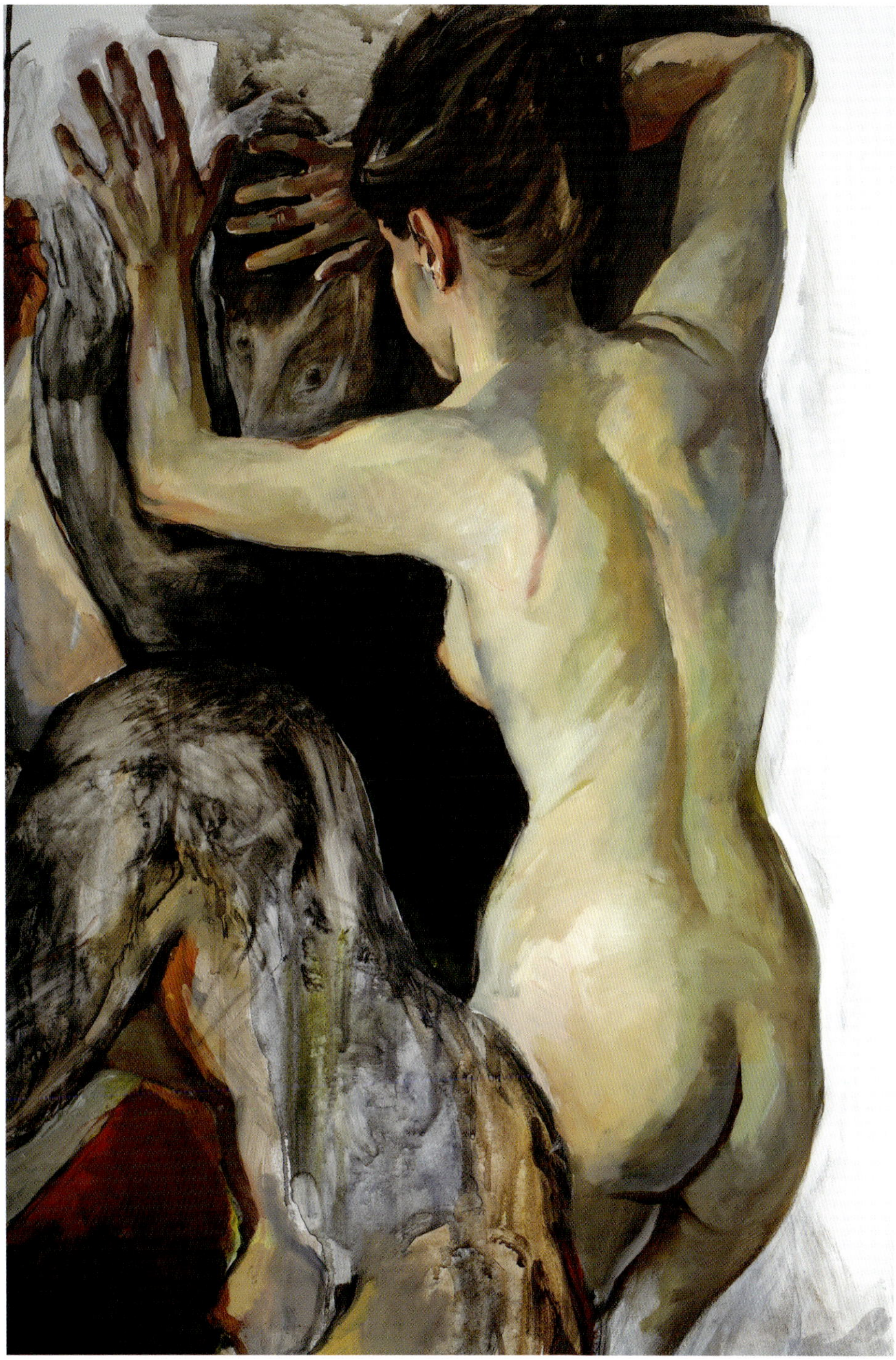

The Fall (Detail 2)

For some time I had in my head images of falling and flying figures. In 2003 I travelled from Rome to Orvieto to visit Orvieto Cathedral and see Luca Signorelli's fresco *The End of the World* (1499–1552). I stayed in the cathedral chapel for hours, studying the expressive, visionary compositions. The Fall evolved gradually without preliminary sketches, working with one life model. The demons and fearful heads reinforce the sense of fear and anxiety.

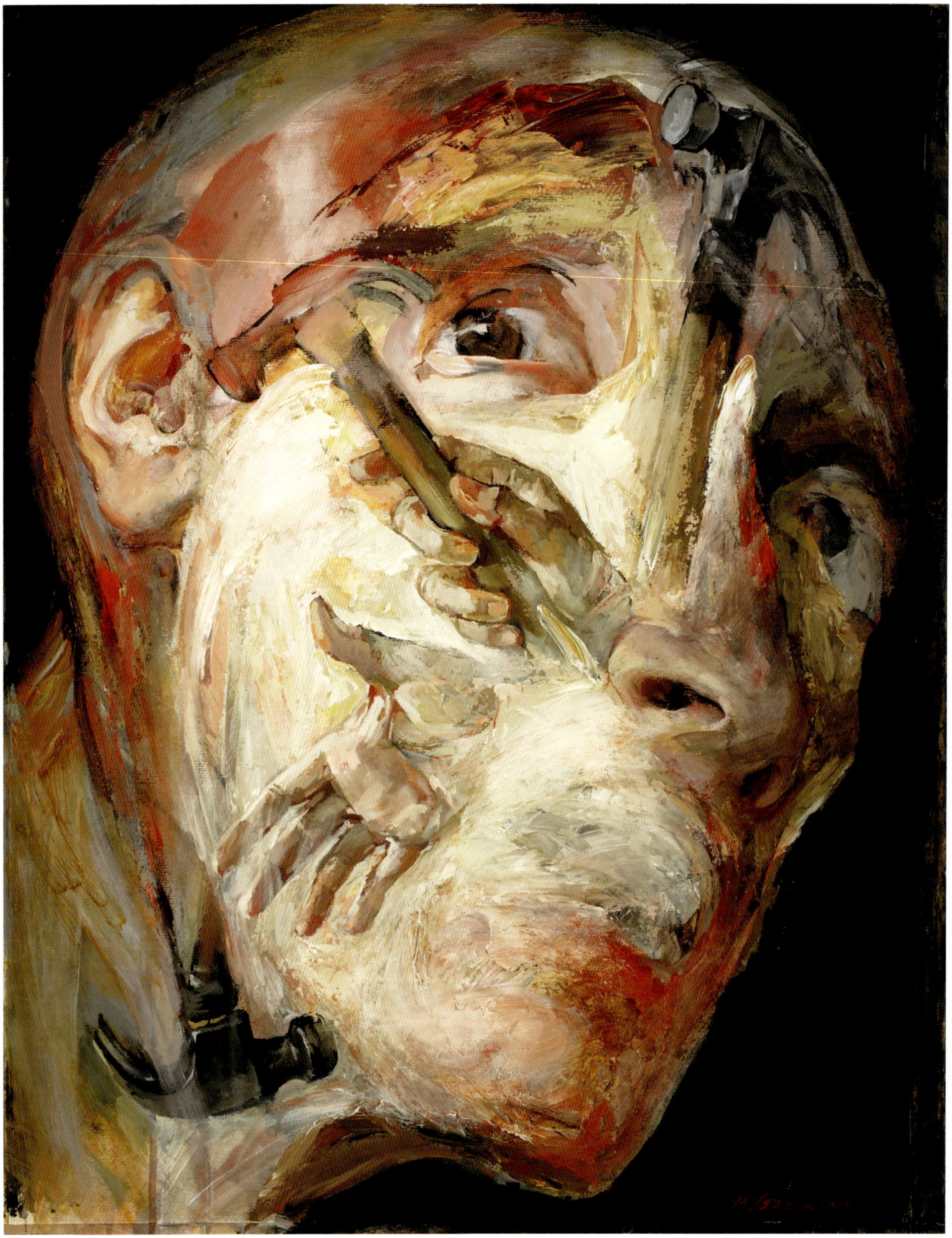

Hammer in the Head

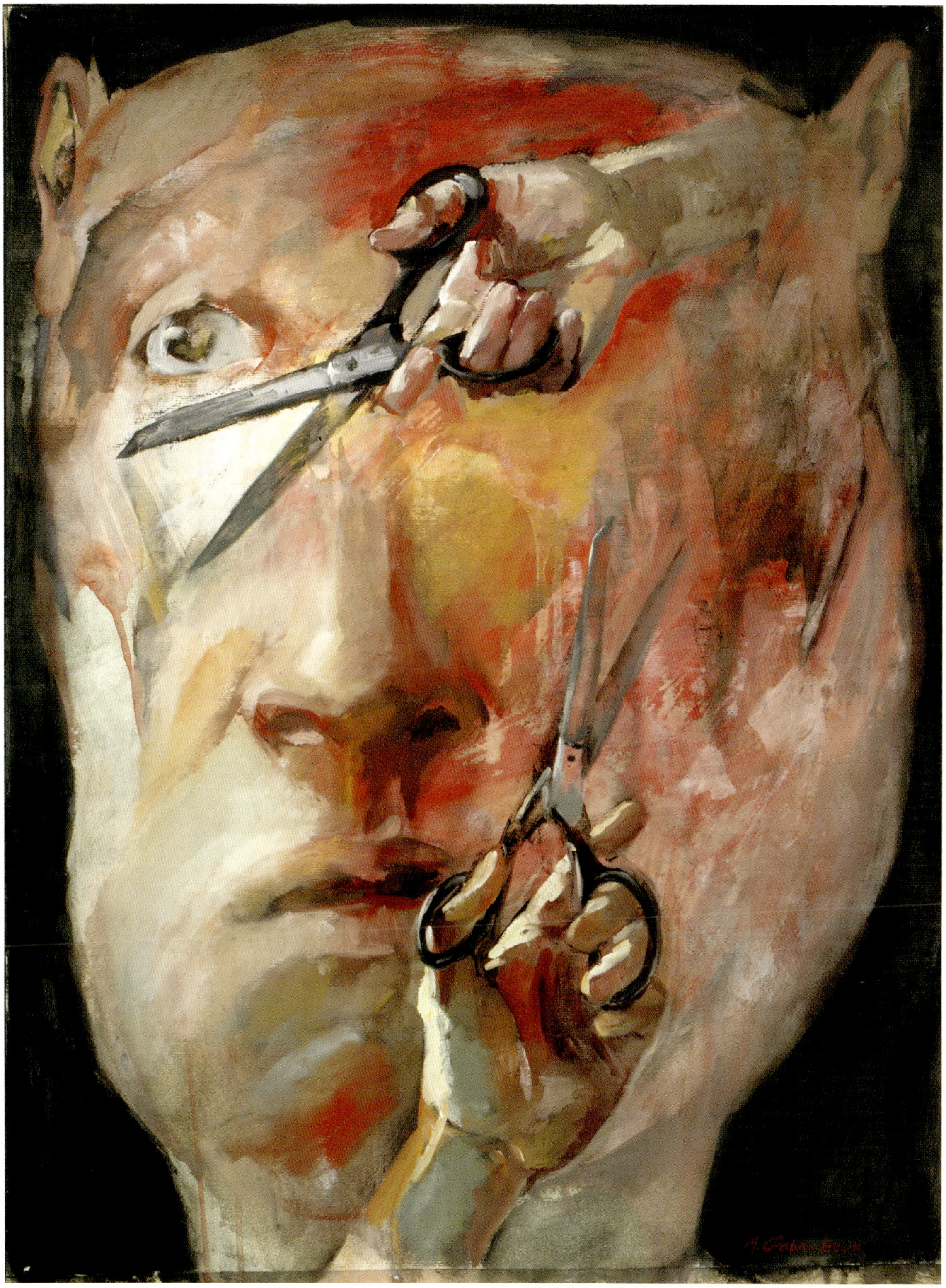

Globalization

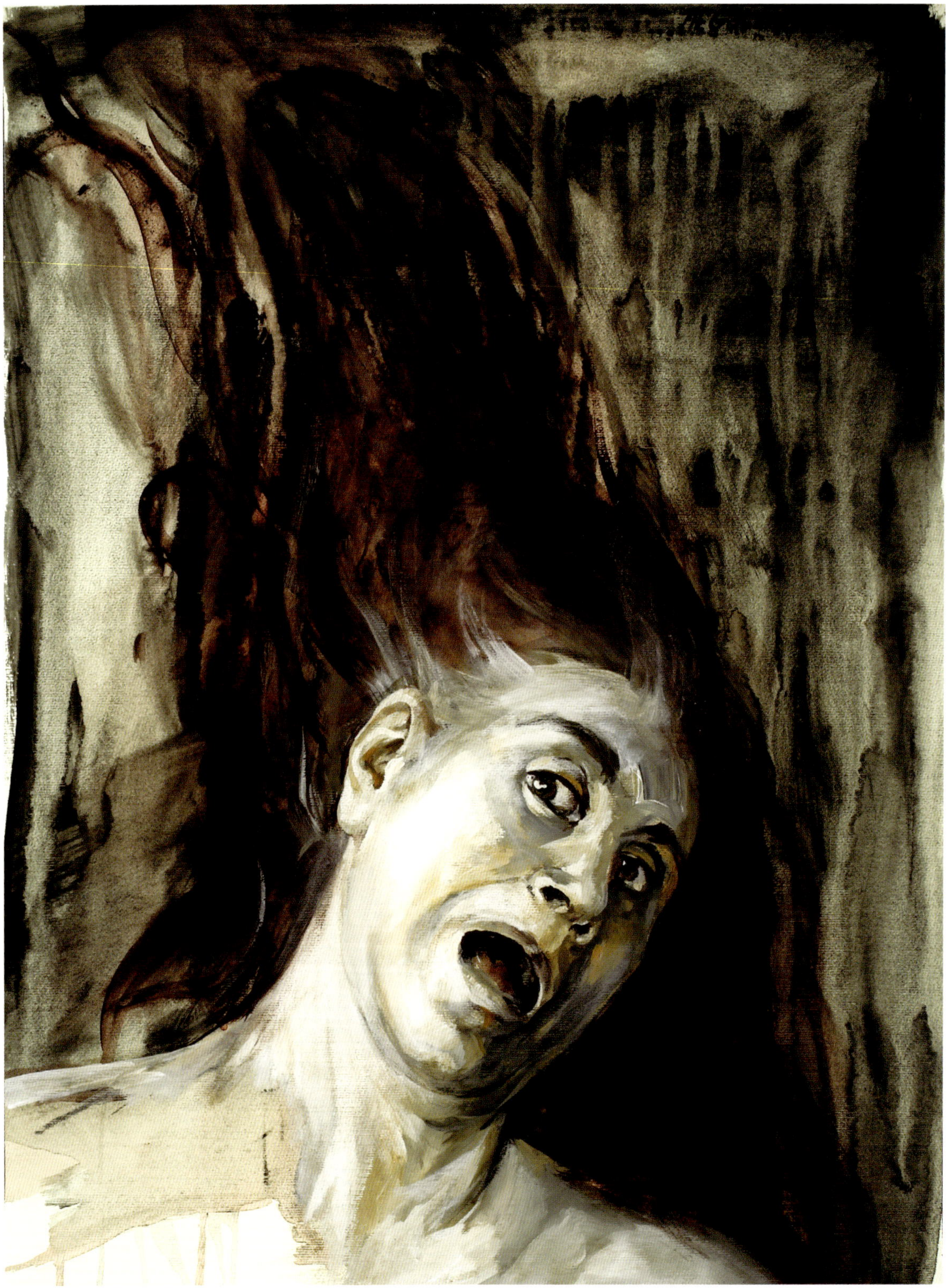

Self-portrait — Fear

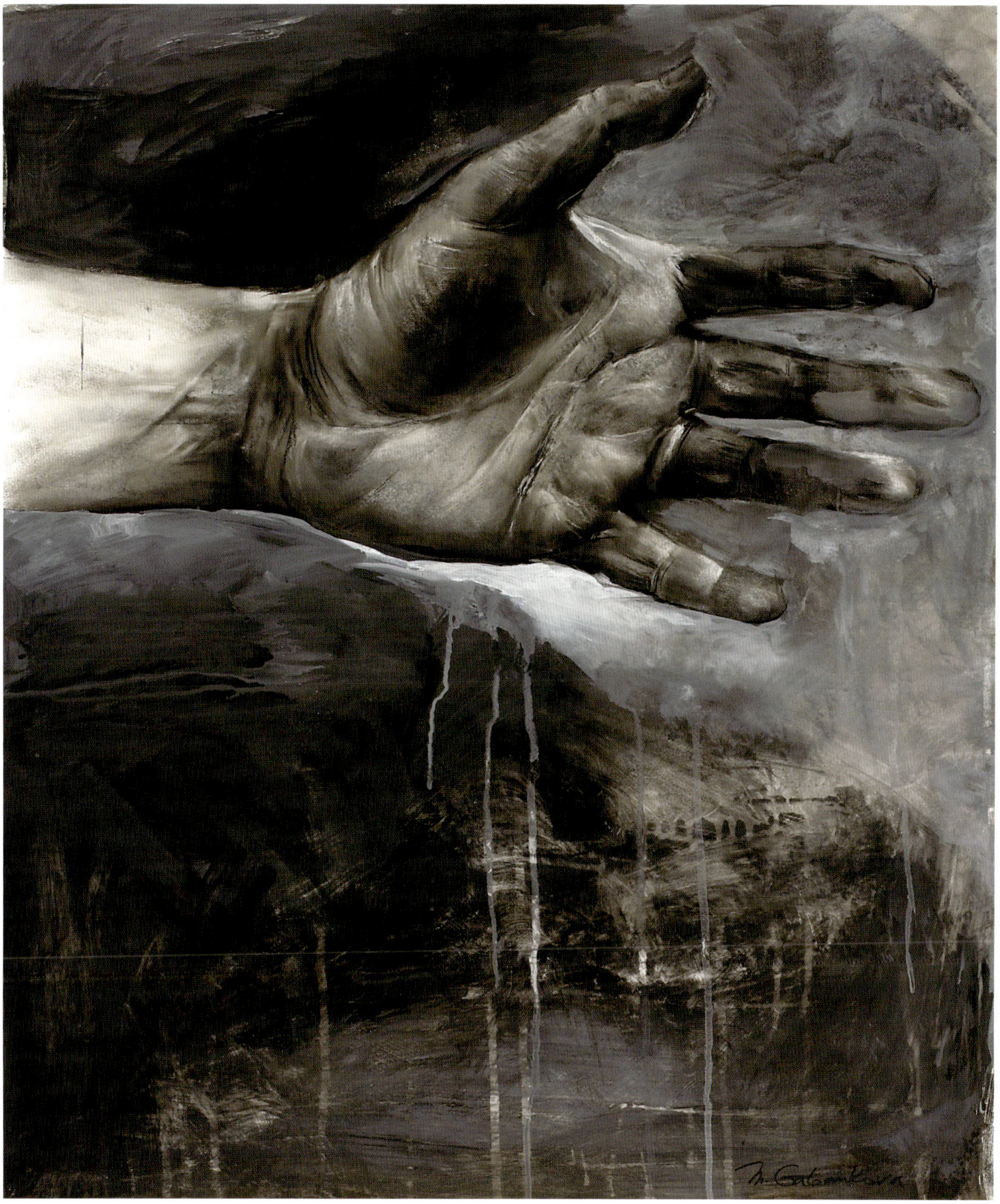

Self-portrait—My Hand

In this larger-than-life drawing, my hand is a symbol of my identity as an artist. It indicates my love of things handmade and of direct tactile involvement with materials, the struggle and messiness of art making, and the wonderful sense of satisfaction found in creativity.

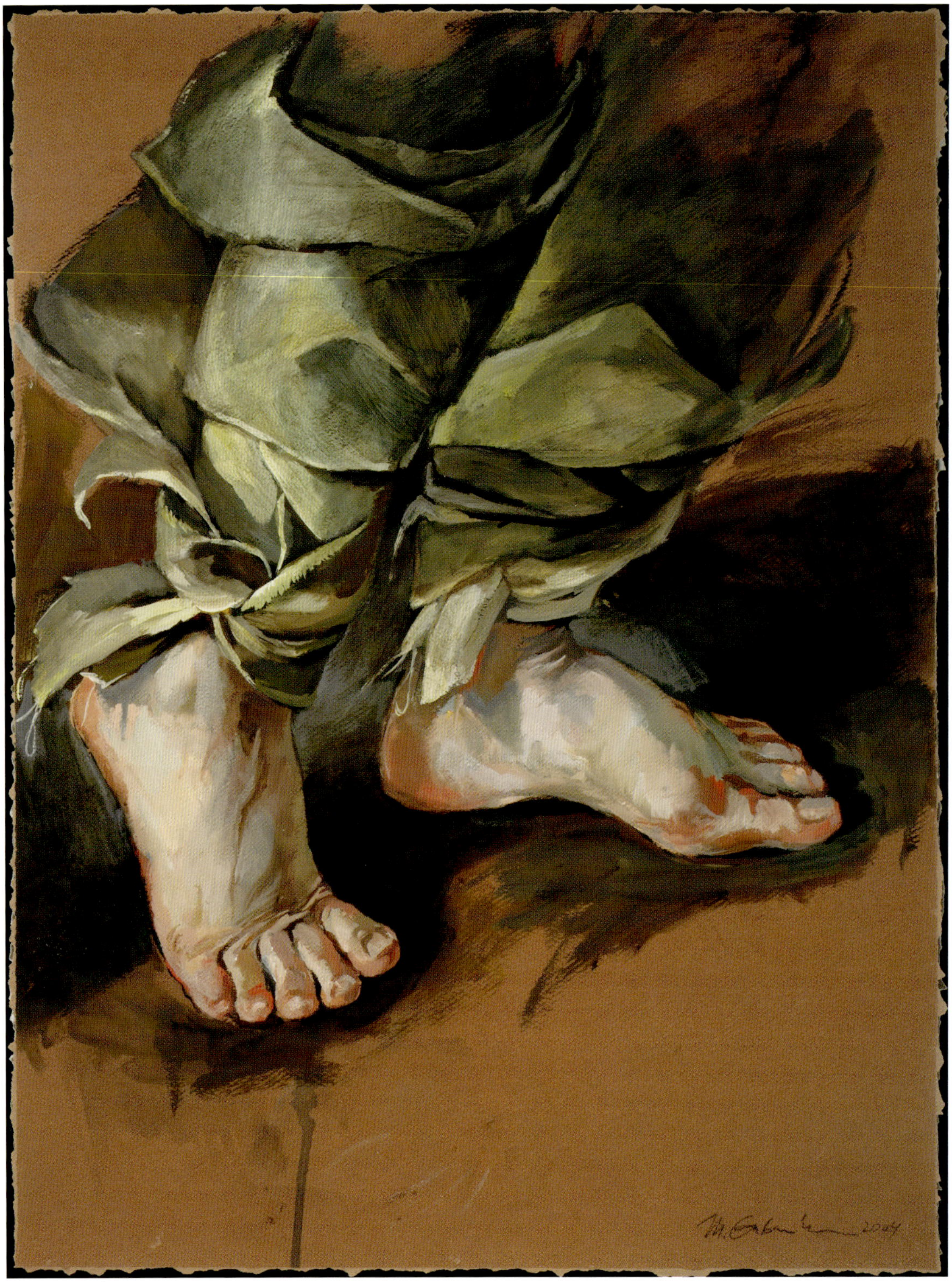

Feet—Good News

'How beautiful are the feet of those who bring good news!' (Rom 10:15)

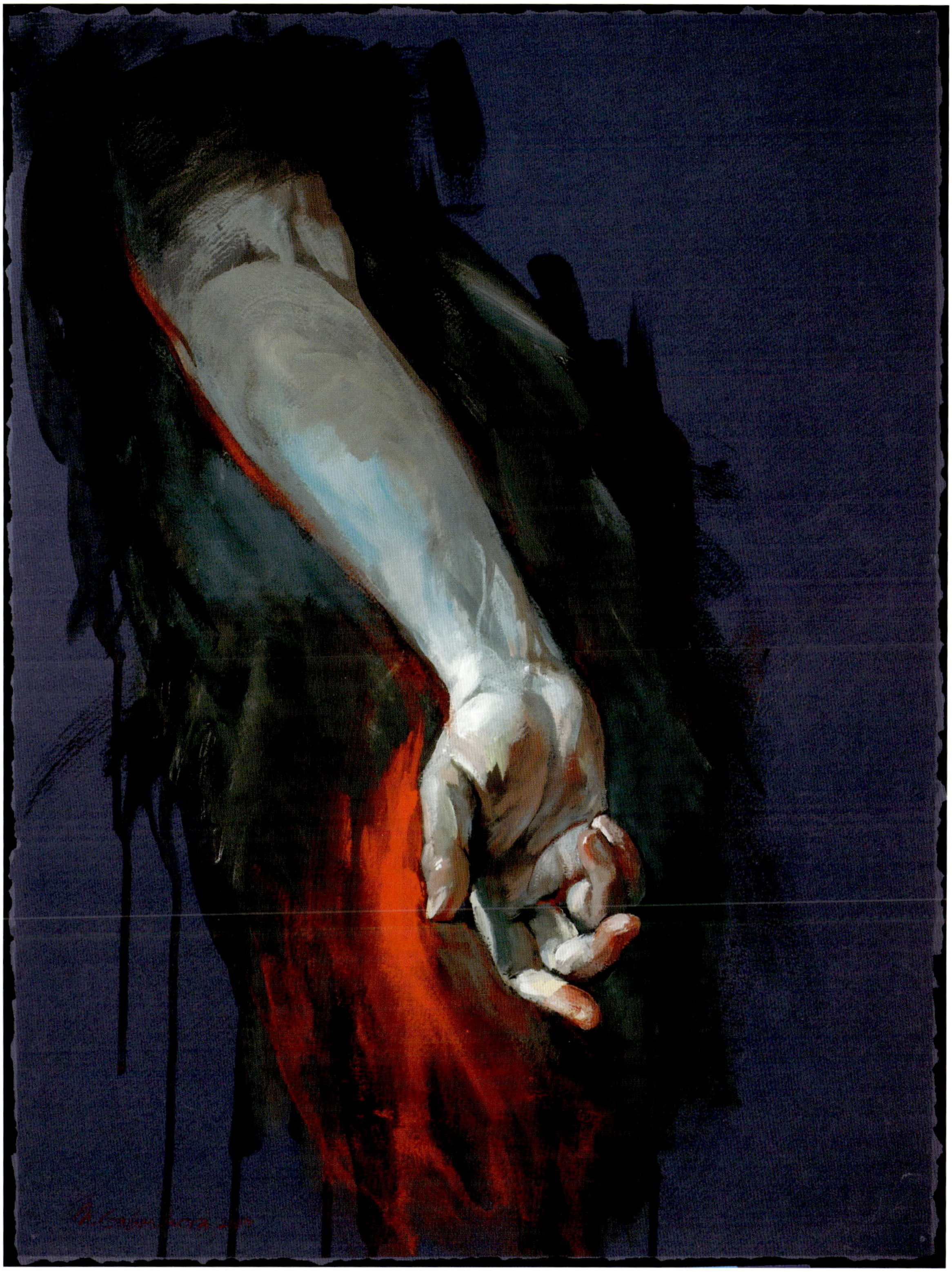

Hand—Grace

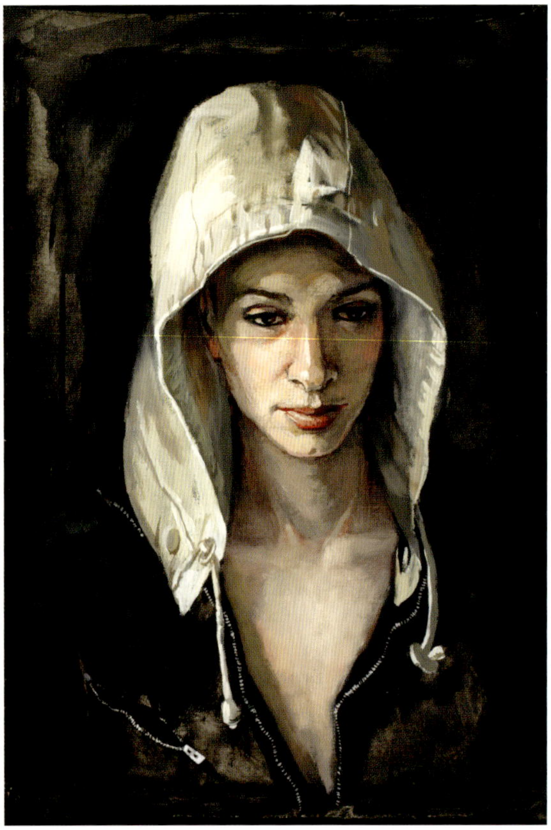

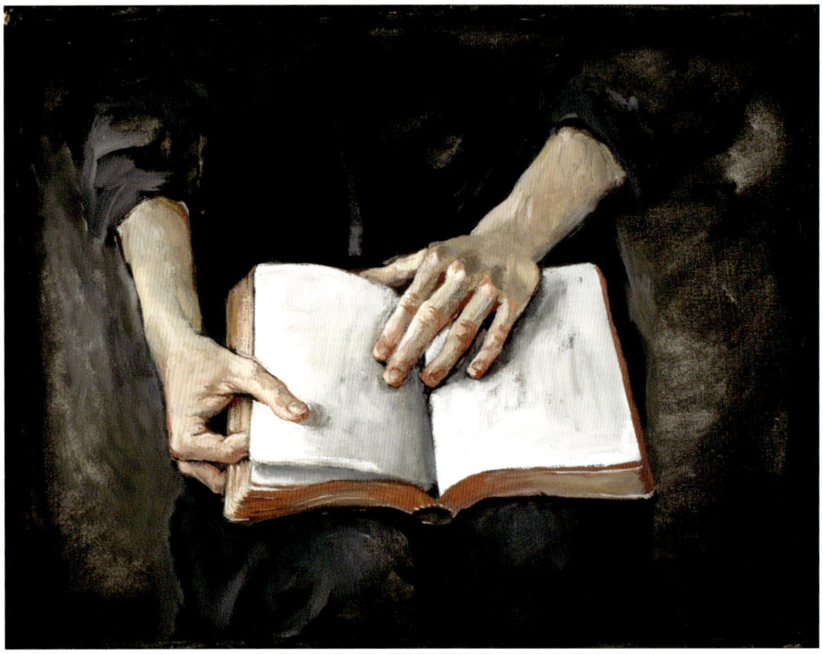

Hope

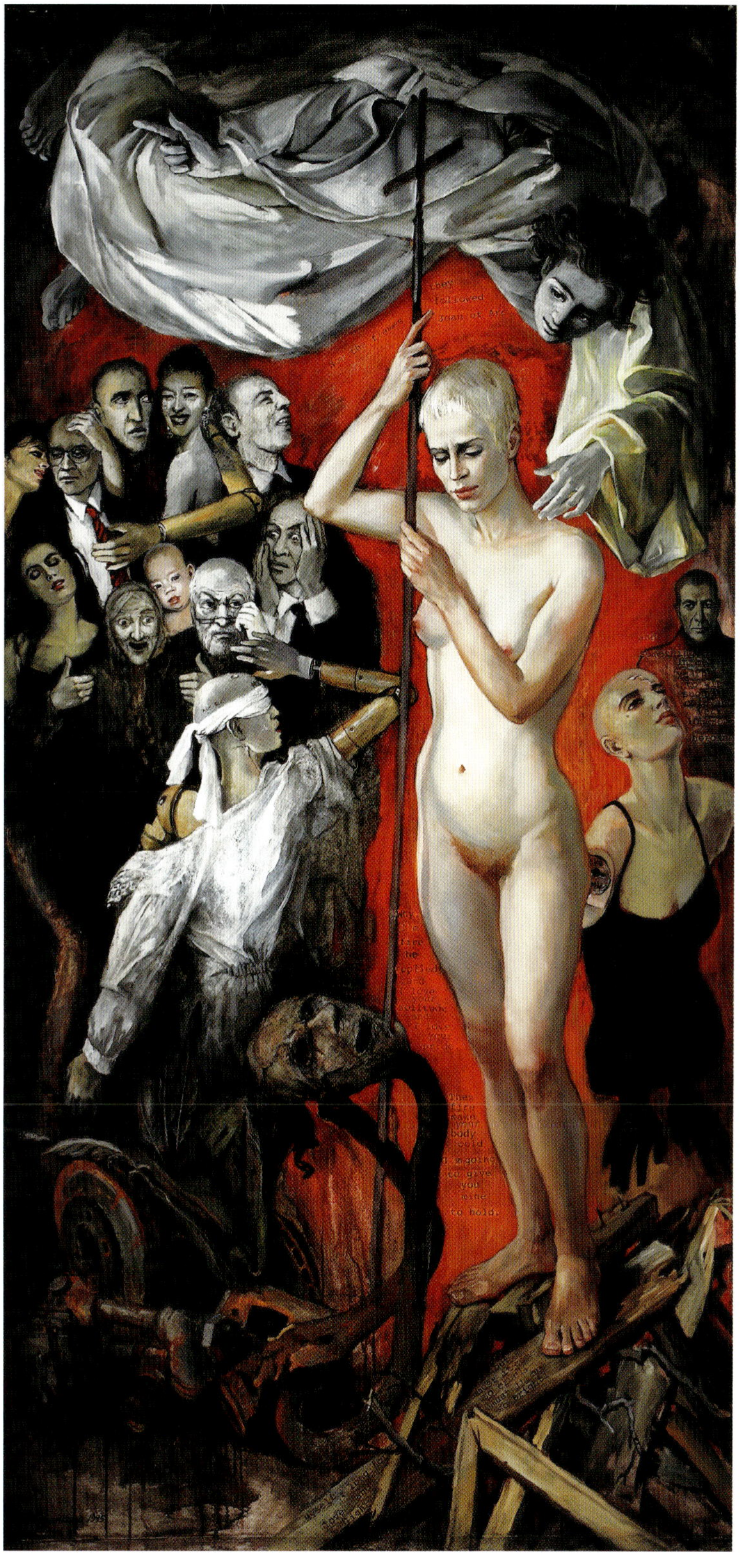

Joan of Arc

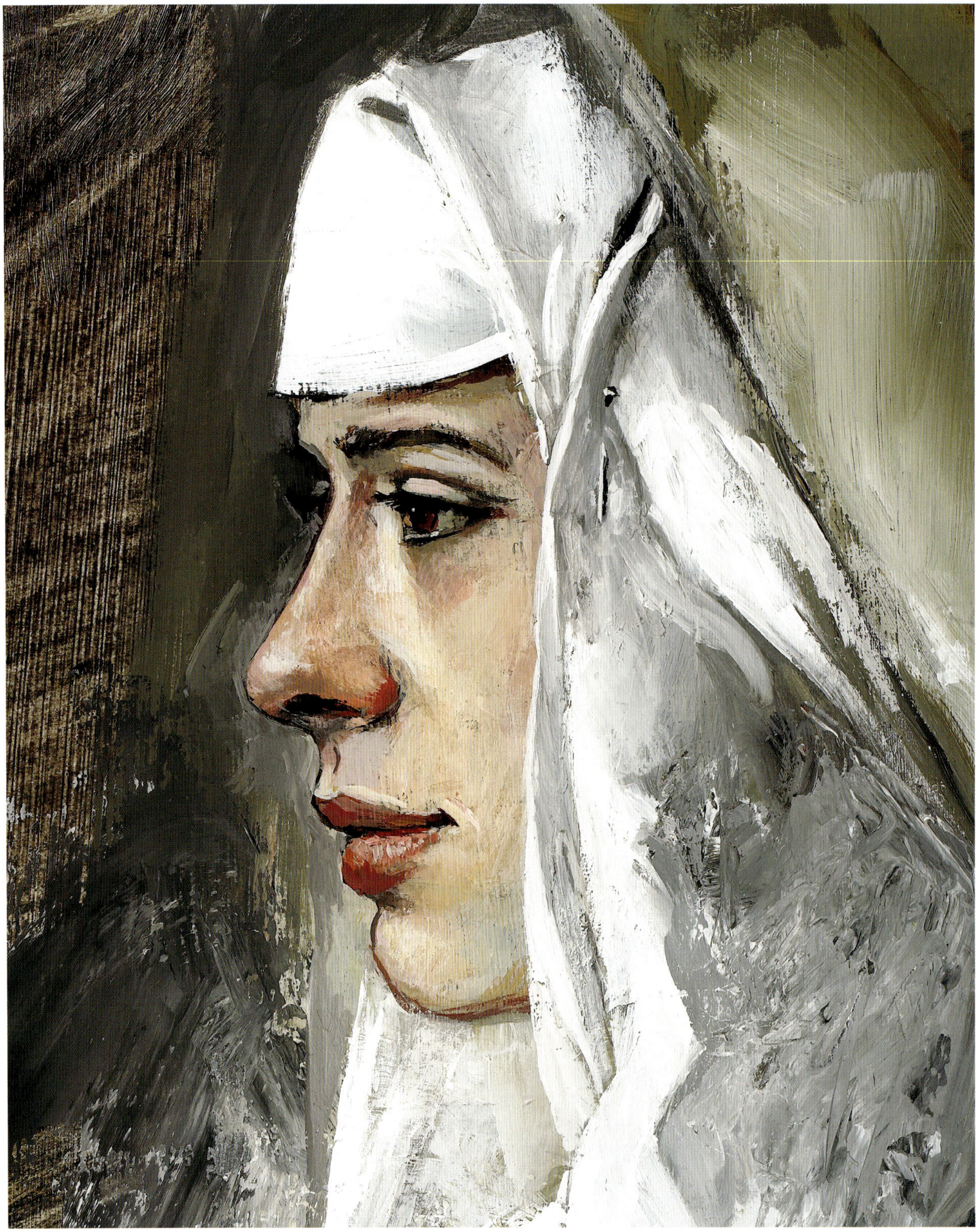

Messengers of Light (Detail)

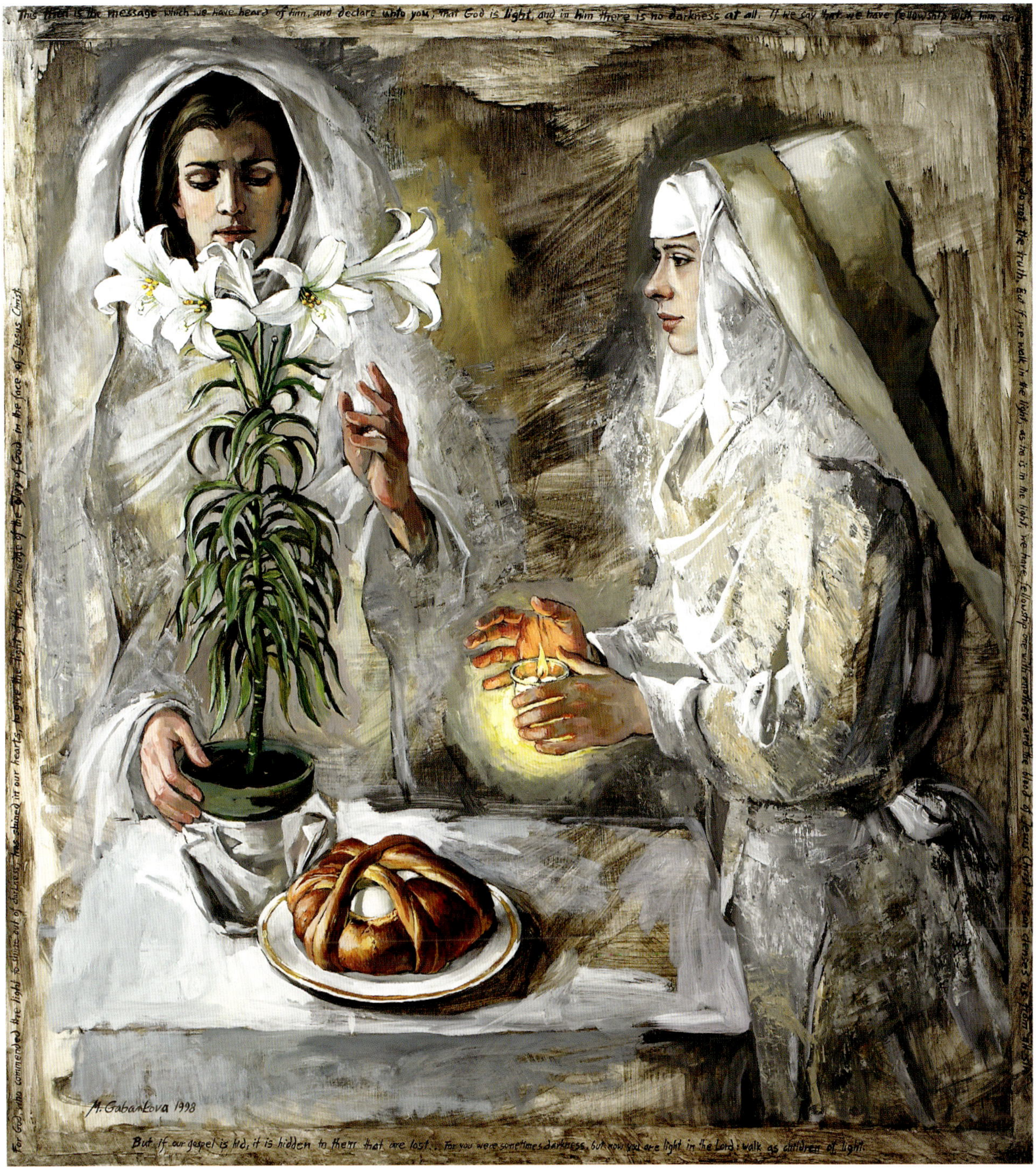

Messengers of Light

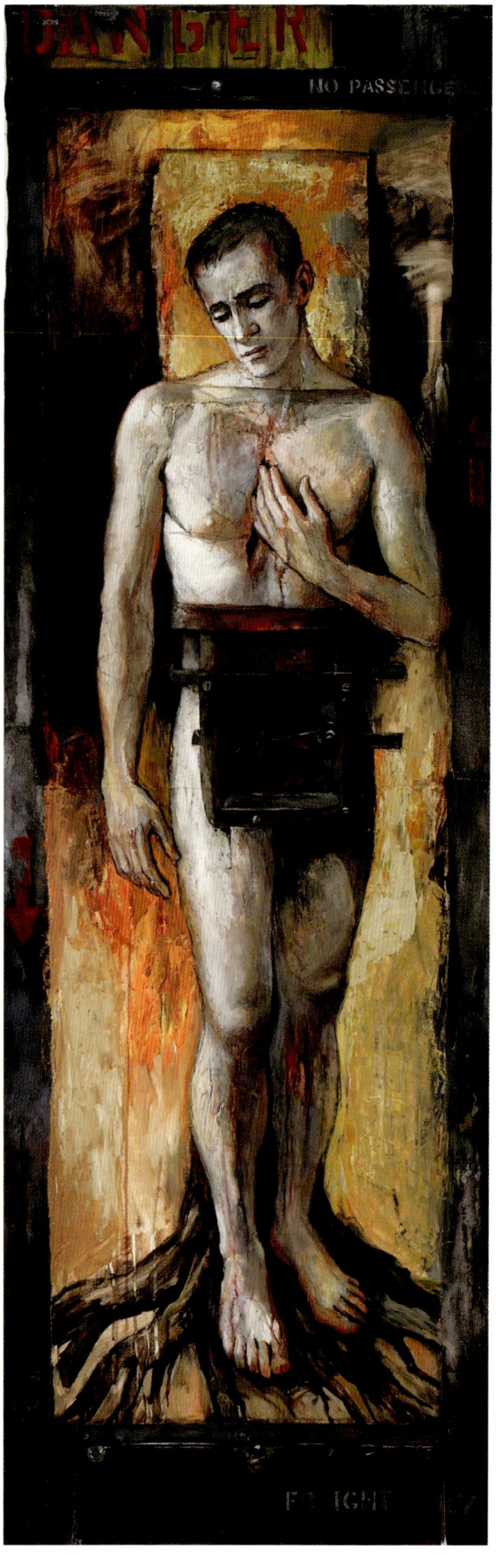

Sebastian

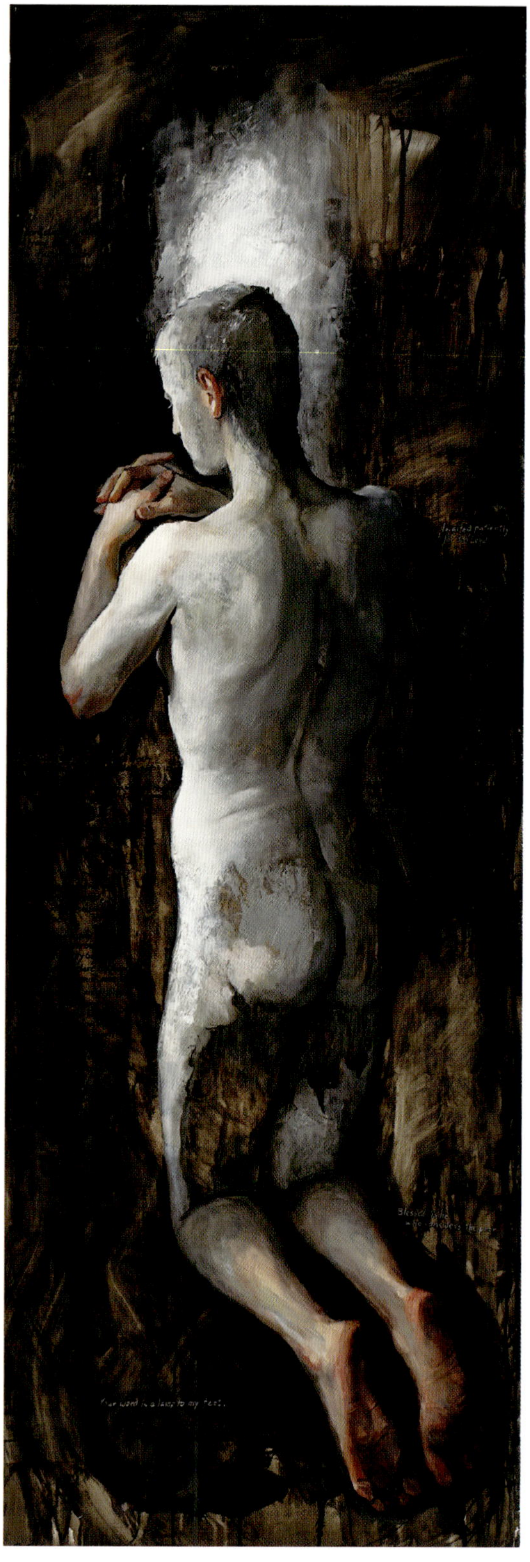

Psalms

Several times in the Bible, God is presented as giving exact instructions for building specific structures. There are also descriptions of an angelic being holding a measuring instrument. Here the callipers and the plumb line held by the figure and the circle behind them symbolize the completeness and unchangeability of God. The figure stands on the Bible—rooted in the Word.

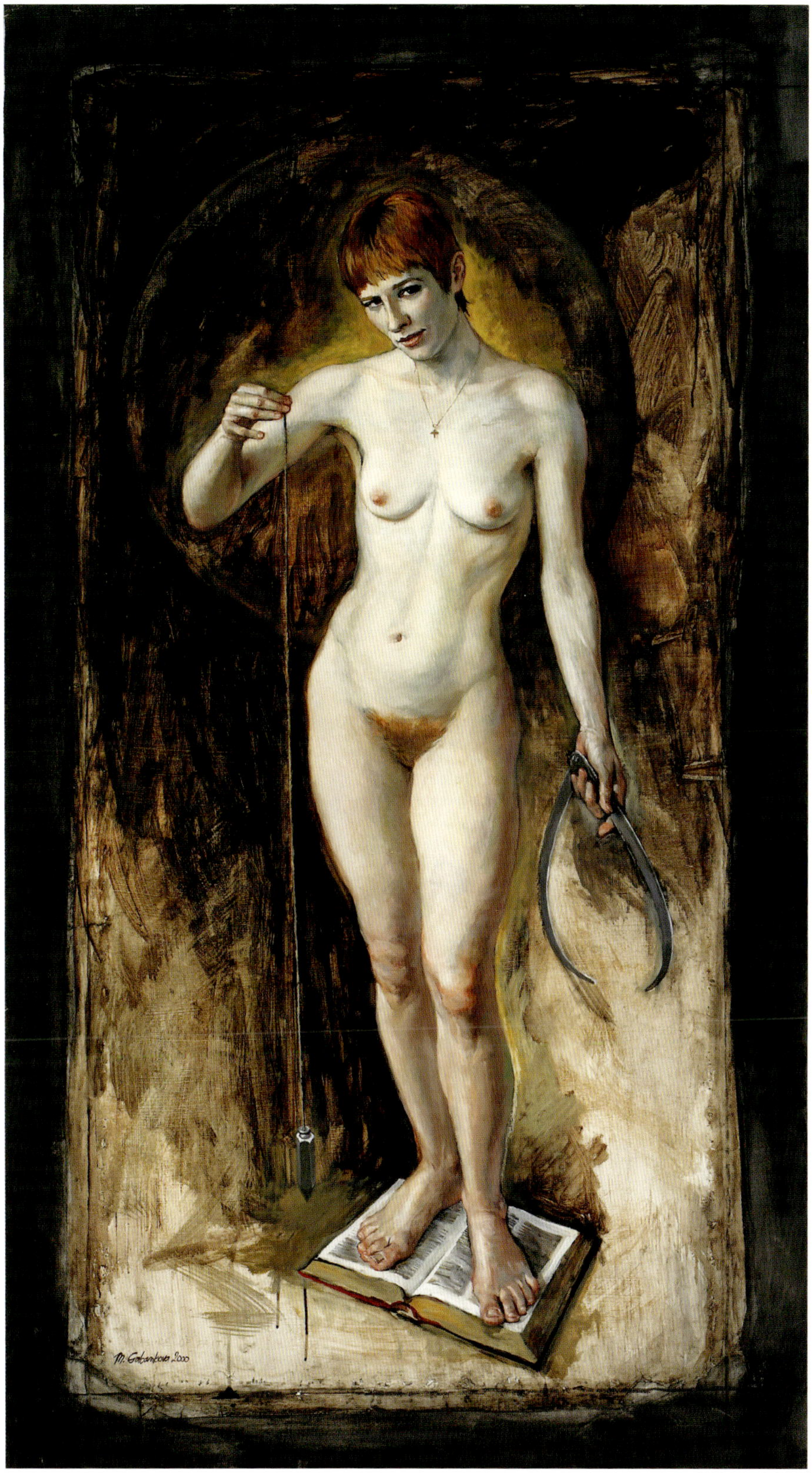

Measure of Faith

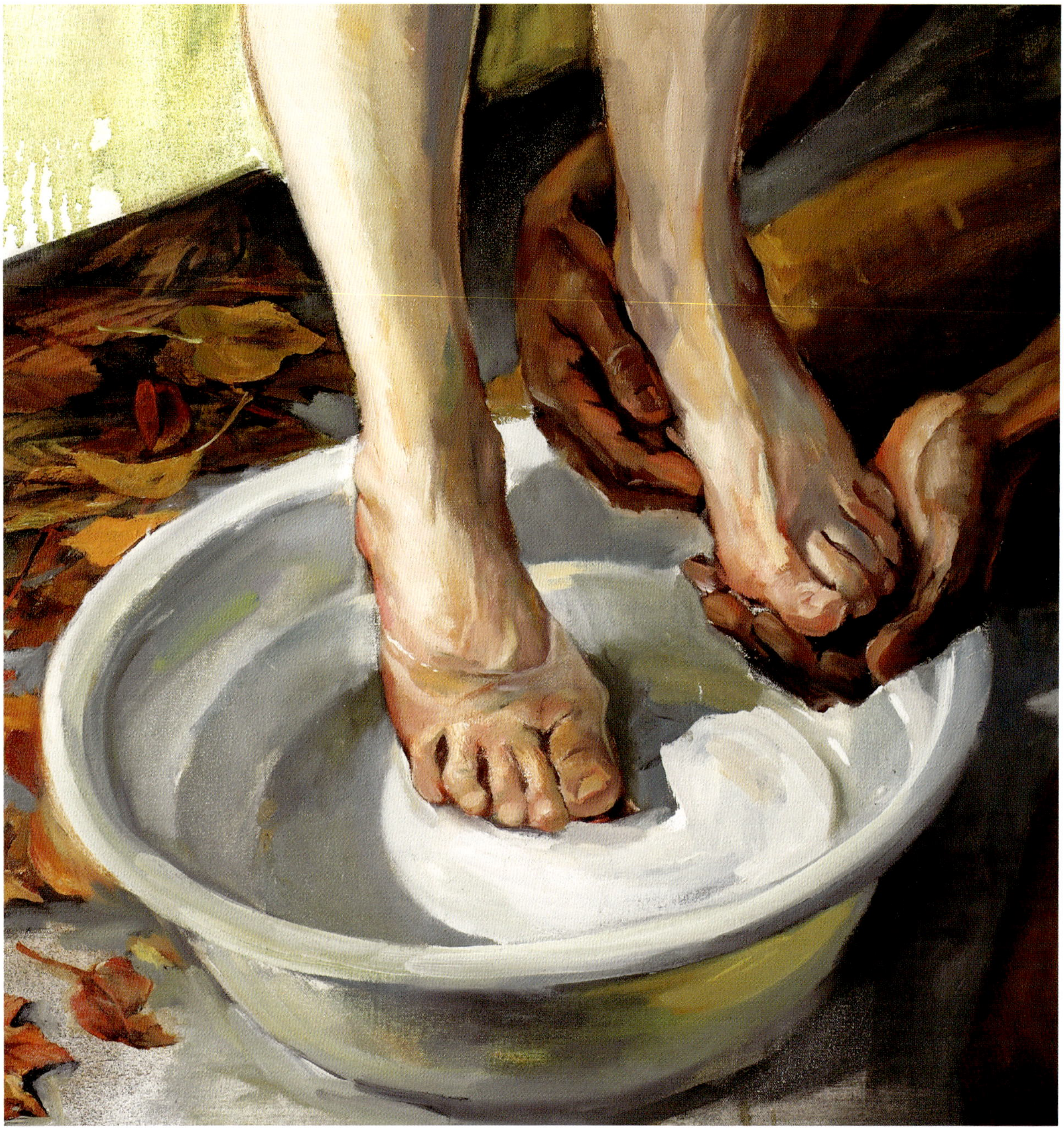

Waiting for a Miracle (Detail 1)

There is a lot going on in this image. The figures on the right, including myself, look towards the left—an unfinished canvas from which emerges a seated female figure having her feet washed by a male figure. The artist actually looks beyond the canvas space onto the real-life models. I am looking for a miracle; I don't want to fail to recognize it when it happens. In the act of foot washing, the miracle of agapé love is manifested among us.

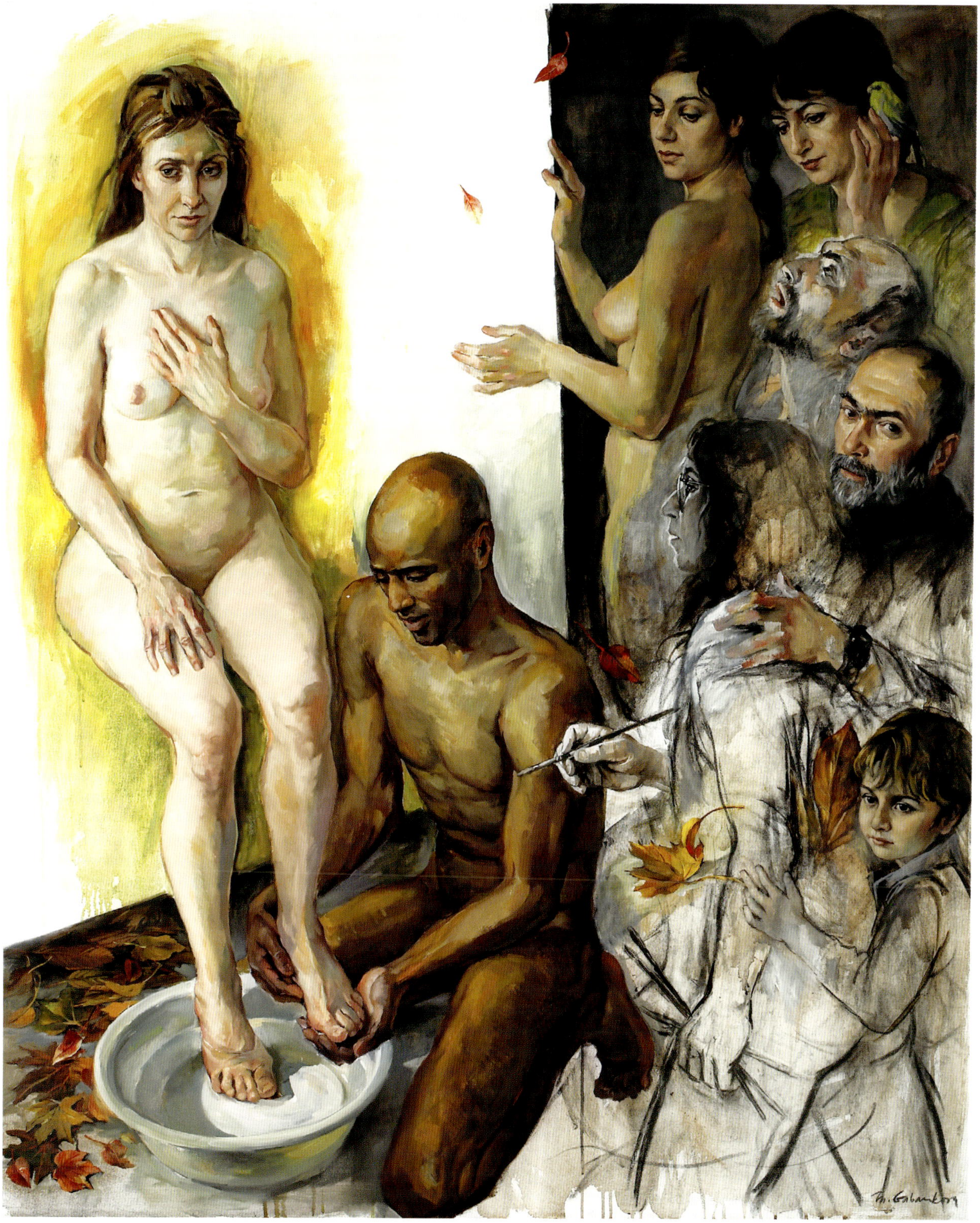

Waiting for a Miracle

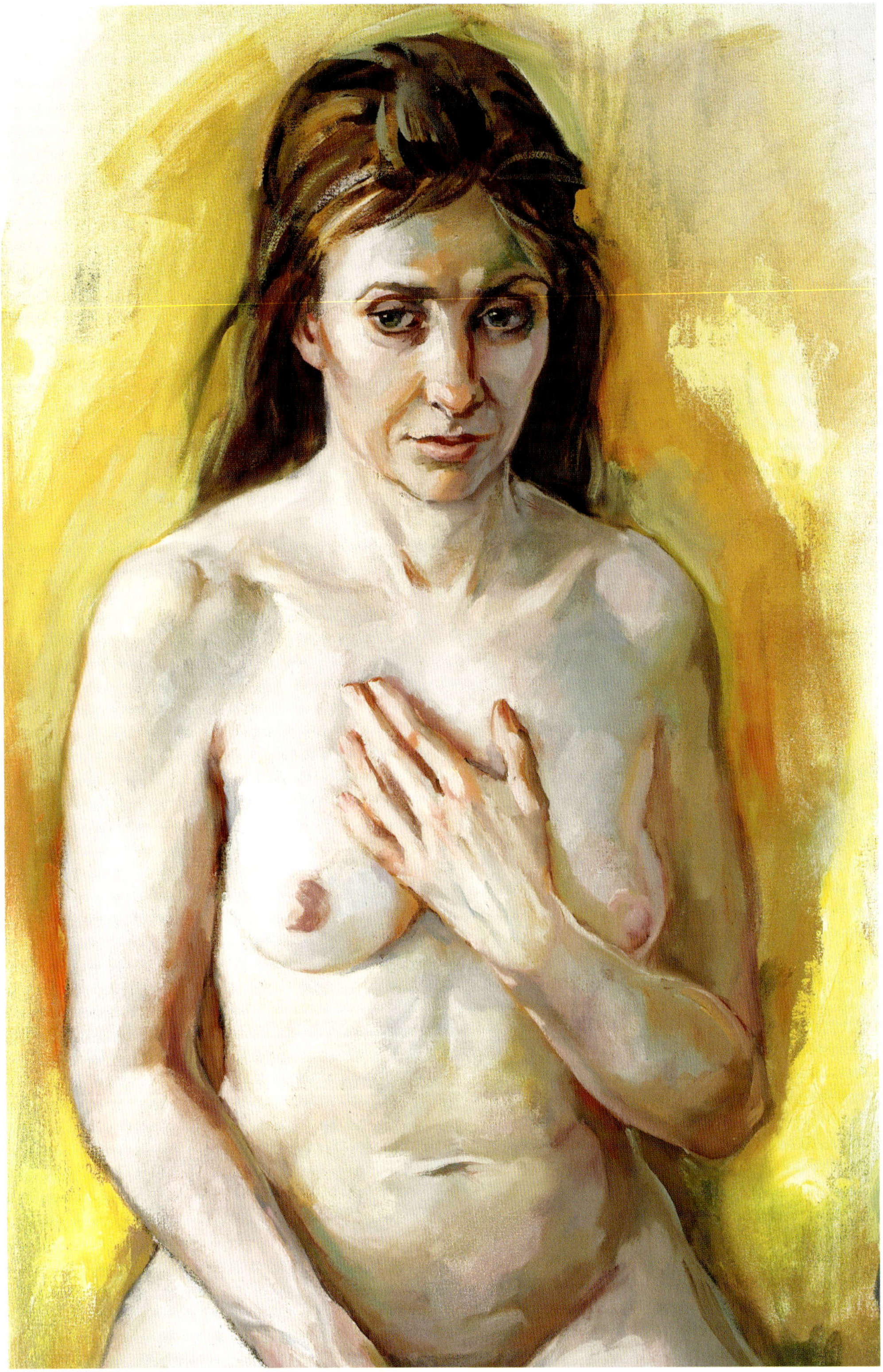

Waiting for a Miracle (Detail 2)

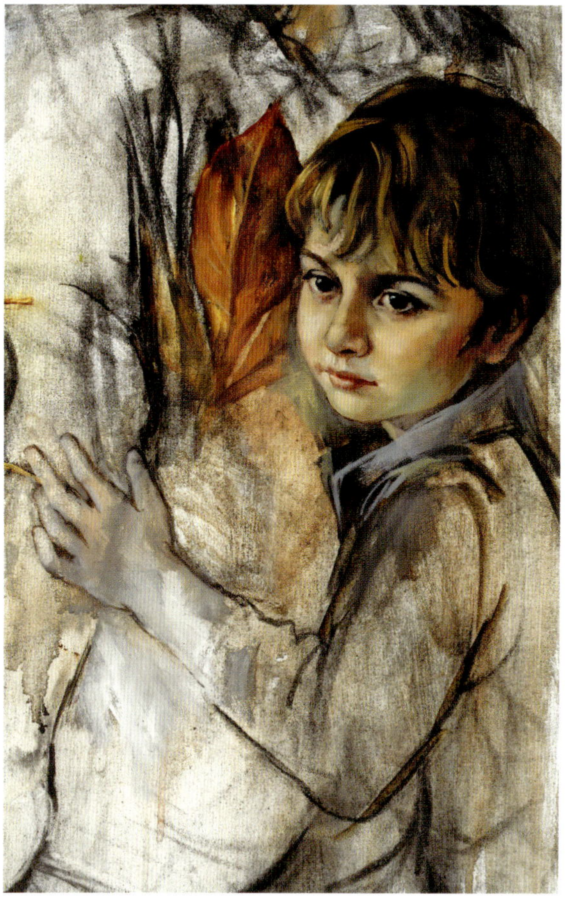

Waiting for a Miracle (Detail 4)

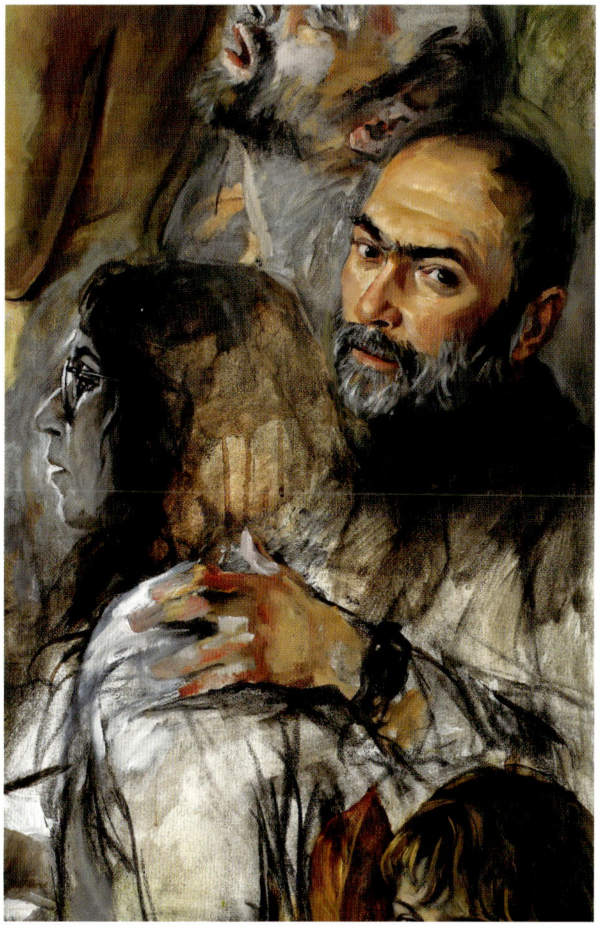

Waiting for a Miracle (Detail 3)

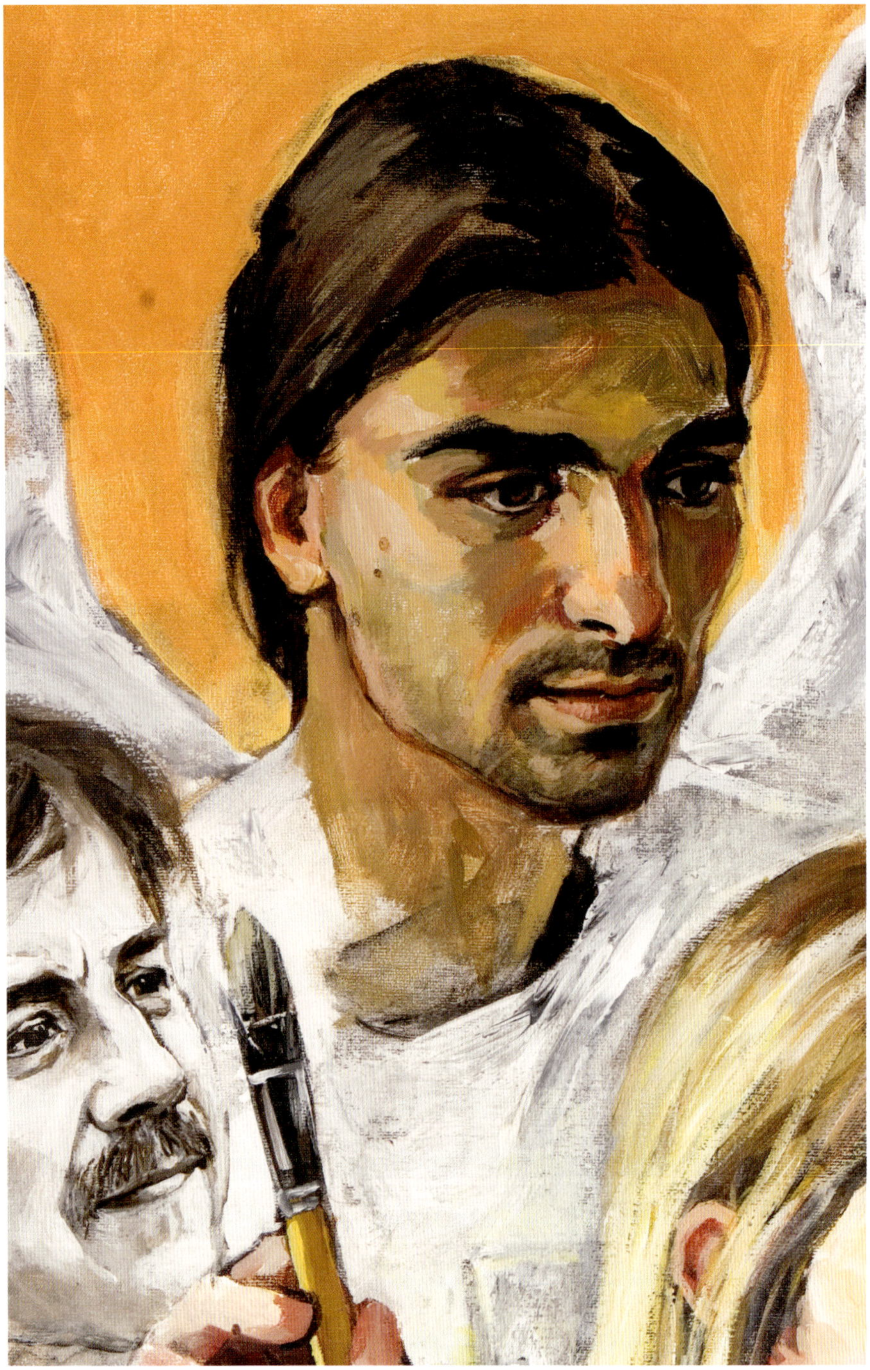

New Song (Detail 1)

In this work I use references from Bible texts as symbols of spiritual realities. Longing for and attaining heaven is represented by attending a banquet. It is my vision of real people—my friends—gathered for a heavenly feast: 'Blessed are those who are invited to the wedding supper of the Lamb' (Rev 19:9). A tree of life grows out of the banquet table. The musical instruments represent the new song of praise to God, and the food and drink symbolize all the marvellous things that God has prepared for the redeemed.

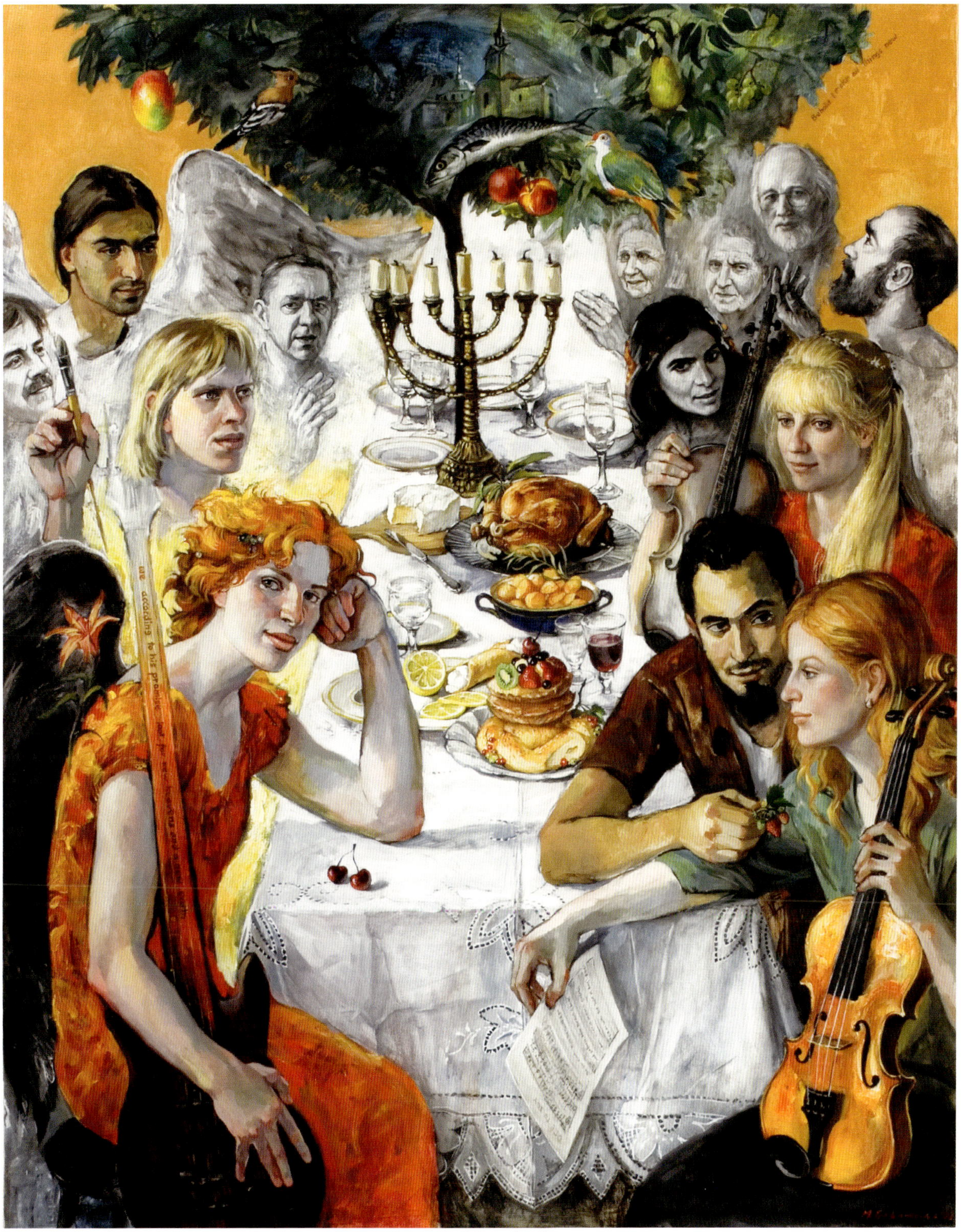

New Song

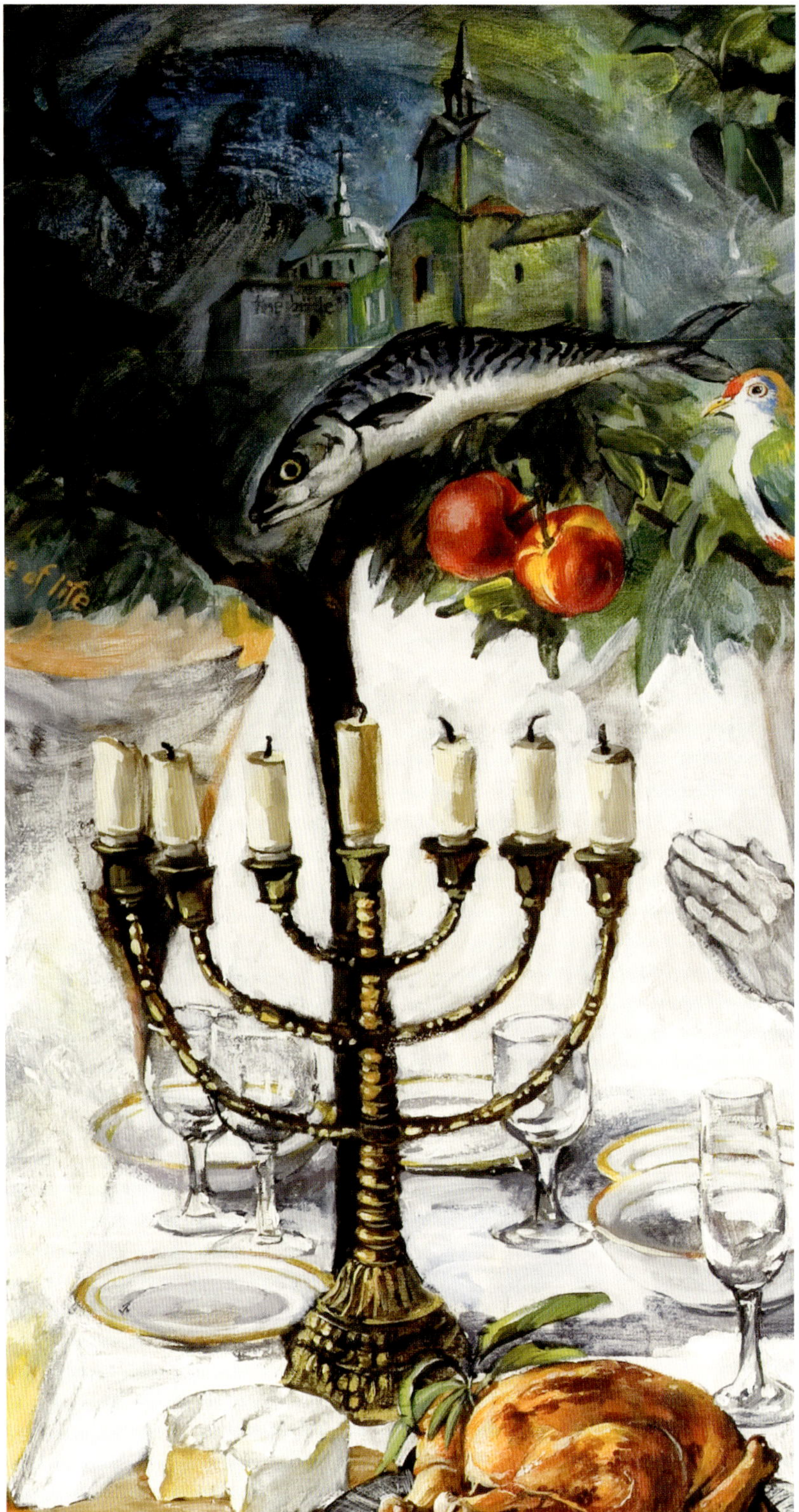

New Song (Detail 2)

Maria Gabankova

b. 18 July 1951 in Ostrava, Czechoslovakia
www.paintinggallery.net

1968	Moves to Vancouver, B.C., Canada
1970–71	Studies at University of British Columbia Department of Fine Arts, Vancouver
1971	Travels to England and Spain
1974	Studies at School of Art and Design, Montreal
1975–77	Studies at Vancouver School of Art. Graduates in printmaking
1975–80	Apprenticeship with artists J Gabanek and A Laník-Gabanek, Vancouver
1979–80	Studies at The Art Students League of New York
1983	Moves to Toronto, Canada
1991	Starts to teach at Ontario College of Art, Toronto
	Marries Aleš Březina
1997	Coordinates Ontario College of Art and Design Florence Programme, Italy
1997–present	Member of Ontario Society of Arts
1998	Artist residency at German Art Foundation in Florence, Italy
2006	Artist residency in Petrovac, Montenegro

Solo Exhibitions

1978	Gallery West, Vancouver
1981	Alex Fraser Gallery, Vancouver
1982	Aries Art Gallery, Ottawa
1984	Waterloo Public Library, Waterloo, Ontario
1985	Gallerie Alexandre, Montreal
1987	The First Canadian Place, Toronto
1991	North York Public Library, Toronto
1993	'Forgotten News', Wilfred Laurier University, Waterloo, Ontario
1994	'Figura non grata', Carnegie Gallery, Dundas, Ontario
1995	'Figura grata', Gallery Bonaventura, Prague, Czech Republic
	'Realism and Resurrection', Regis College, University of Toronto
1996	'Figures', St James Cathedral, Toronto
	'Body of Dust', The Lookout Gallery, Regent College, Vancouver
1997	'Inner Being', Newman Centre, Toronto
1998	'Inner Being II', Tyndale College, Toronto
	'Sogno La Specola', Villa Romana, Florence, Italy
1999	Joseph Workman Auditorium, Toronto
2000	'As in a Mirror Dimly', Augustine College, Ottawa
2001	'6981 km from Toronto', Galerie Michalský dvor, Bratislava, Slovakia
	'Incongruous Conjunctions—Report from a Leaking Boat', Loop Gallery, Toronto
2002	'Con Fuoco', Hamilton Conservatory for the Arts, Hamilton, Ontario
	'Eyedentity', Loop Gallery, Toronto
2003	'New Work', Loop Gallery, Toronto
2004	'the body redeemed', Redeemer University College, Ancaster, Ontario
2005	'the body broken', Institute for Christian Studies, Toronto
	'Between the Word and Flesh', Loop Gallery, Toronto

Selected Group Exhibitions

1975–90	Participates in twenty group exhibitions across North America
1990	Karney Gallery and Louise Smith Gallery, Toronto
1991	Ontario College of Art, Faculty Show, Toronto
1992	Two exhibitions at Karney Gallery, Toronto
	'Art Credo'. 3rd Prize Award, Toronto

1994	'POSSE'. Toronto
	Pastel Society of Canada. 2nd Prize Award, Ottawa
	'Art Credo'. 1st Prize Award, Toronto
	Ontario College of Art, Faculty Exhibition, Toronto
	Society of Canadian Artists show. Jury Award
1995	'95' Yoo Kyung International Exhibition of Drawing'. Seoul, South Korea
1997	Junction Arts Festival, Toronto
	CIVA conference, Juried exhibition. Montreal
	Ontario College of Art and Design, Florence, Italy
1999	'Through the Glass Brightly'. Wycliffe College, Toronto
	'Canadian Spaces'. The North American Centre of Oriental Arts, Toronto
2000	'Representations'. Ontario Society of Artists, Lieutenant Governor Suite, Queens Park, Toronto
	'Evidence of things not seen'. Tyndale College, Toronto
	'Into Body'. Ontario Society of Artists, F H Varley Art Gallery, Unionville, Ontario
2002	Canadian Opera and Canadian National Ballet, Hummingbird Centre, Toronto
2002	'New Heaven—New Earth'. Painted City, Toronto
2003	'New Heaven—New Earth'. Look Out Gallery, Vancouver
2004	Loop Gallery, Toronto
2005	'Art Canada 5'. Czech Ministry of Culture, New City Hall, Prague, Czech Republic
	'Portrait! Who and What are you?' Varley Gallery, Unionville, Ontario
	'Exploring the Threshold, Art and Theology in Dialogue'. Toronto School of Theology
2006	'Spirit and Creation'. Wycliffe College, University of Toronto
	'Suffering and Glory'. Trinity Anglican Church, Cambridge, Ontario
	'Fragility and Hope'. International AIDS Conference, St James Cathedral, Toronto
	International Biennale of Nudes. Petrovac, Montenegro

Selected Commissions

Maria Gabankova has painted commissioned portraits in North America for many well-known personalities, such as the Czech-Canadian novelists Josef Škvorecký and Zdena Salivarová, Czech poet Karel Kryl, Canadian pianist Antonín Kubálek, composer Oskar Morawetz, Knox College principal Dr J D Corbett, Presbyterian College professors J McLelland and W Klempa of McGill University, Montreal, NHL hockey player Miroslav Fryčer and world ice-skating champion Aja Vrzáňová.

1995–2000	Work for film productions *Gossip* (Warner Brothers), *Three to Tango* (Warner Brothers), *Catwalk* (TV Series)
2003	Copy of the Isenheim Alterpiece's Crucifixion panel by M Grünewald for the Biblical Museum of Canada, Vancouver, B.C.
2004	Portrait of Mrs F Parkin, Principal of Harbord Collegiate, Toronto
2005	Portrait of Honourable Ch Mayer, former Canadian Minister of Agriculture, Canadian Agricultural Hall of Fame, Toronto
2006	Portrait of Mr Peter Hannam, Canadian Agricultural Hall of Fame, Toronto

Selected Public and Corporate Collections

Canadian Agricultural Hall of Fame
Thomas Fisher Rare Book Library, University of Toronto
Humberside Collegiate, Toronto
Recochem Inc. Montreal, Quebec
Bombardier, Montreal, Quebec
Presbyterian College, McGill University, Montreal
Knox College, University of Toronto
Newman Centre, University of Toronto
Prague Castle, President of Czech Republic, Office
German Art Foundation, Villa Romana, Florence, Italy
Biblical Museum of Canada, Vancouver
Harbord Collegiate, Toronto

Selected Bibliography

'The Czechoslovaks.' The *Vancouver Sun*, 25 July 1979
'Studies in Black and White.' The *Chelsea Clinton News* (New York), 14 February 1980
'The New Romantics.' Art Speak (New York), 12 April 1980
'New York Realities.' Art Speak (New York), 8 May 1980
'Putting Life on Line.' The *Vancouver Sun*, 9 April 1983
Interview on the French CBC Radio. Vancouver, September 1983
Interviews on the Radio Free Europe and Voice of America. 1984
Interview on Radio Canada International. Montreal, 1985
Painting Canada, 60 min. documentary for CBC, 1 July 1987
Czech TV documentary, 1993
Interview by Z Salivarová. *Vlasta* magazine, 1993
Jeff Mahon. 'Figura non grata.' *The Spectator*, review of exhibition in Carnegie Gallery, Dundas, Ontario, 1994
Sheila Robertson. 'Art probes body for Presence of Soul.' *Star Phoenix* (Saskatoon) 26 August 1995
Megan Mueller. 'Maria Gabankova: Making Monsters.' *Art Focus* (Toronto) Winter 1995
Canadian Art: Reviews by Betty Ann Jordan, 1995
Nikki Abraham. 'The Art of M. Gabankova: an invitation to Contemplation.' *Catholic New Times*, 1996
Sue Careless. 'Art Talks, Do we Listen?' *Christian Week*, 1999
'6981 km from Toronto' Reviewed in Slovak Daily newspapers *Sme* and *Pravda*, on Slovak TV and Slovak Radio, Bratislava, Slovakia, 2001
Anna Lisa Rapana. 'Viaggio nell'arte del corpo umano.' *Corriere Canadese*, Toronto, 23 February 2001
'Documentary on New Work' Exhibition at Loop Gallery, Nový záběr television, TV OMNI 1, Toronto, 2003, 2004, 2006
'Art Canada 5' reviews in Czech daily newspapers *Právo* and *Lidové noviny* and bi-weekly Toronto-based *Satellite 1-416*, 2005
'Reflections', *Presbyterian Record*, Toronto, February 2006
Milena Katz. 'Shining lights from Eastern Europe.' *Parkhurst Exchange*, April 2006
Mirko Petricevic. 'Illuminating the Word.' *The Record* (Kitchener-Waterloo/Cambridge) 15 April 2006

Published Reproductions of Work

Ivan Klíma. *Moje první lásky*. Toronto: 68 Publishers, 1985, cover
The *Canadian Banker*, March and July issues 1988, covers
Policy Options, 1988, cover
Janis Rapoport. *Upon her fluent route*. 1991, cover and illustrations
'Perfect Bodies'. *Regeneration Quarterly* (Cambridge, MA, USA, 1999) pp14, 15
'What's On'. *Toronto Star*, 8 November 2001
Portrait of Gordon Skilling in 'Profile' sections of *The Globe and Mail*, Toronto and *Mladá fronta Dnes* daily, Czech Republic, 2001
Gordon Skilling. *The Education of a Canadian*. McGill: Queens University Press, 2001, cover
Glorious Hope, September 2000, May 2001, January February 2002, March–April 2003, May–June 2006, covers

Academic Appointments

1976–79	Drawing, painting, printmaking courses at Burnaby Art Centre and at Malaspina Printmakers Society, Vancouver
1981–83	Drawing and painting at Fraser Valley College, Abbotsford
1985–90	Continuing education art courses and workshops in Seneca College, Etobicoke Art Centre, Toronto and Burlington Art Centre, Burlington, Ontario
1996	Course in Figure and Drapery, Realist Academy, Seattle, WA, USA
1998–2002	MFA in Drawing and Painting programme, Norwich University, Vermont, artist teacher
2004	Redeemer University College, Ancaster, Ontario
1990–present	Associate Professor at Ontario College of Art and Design, Faculty of Art: Drawing and Painting, Toronto

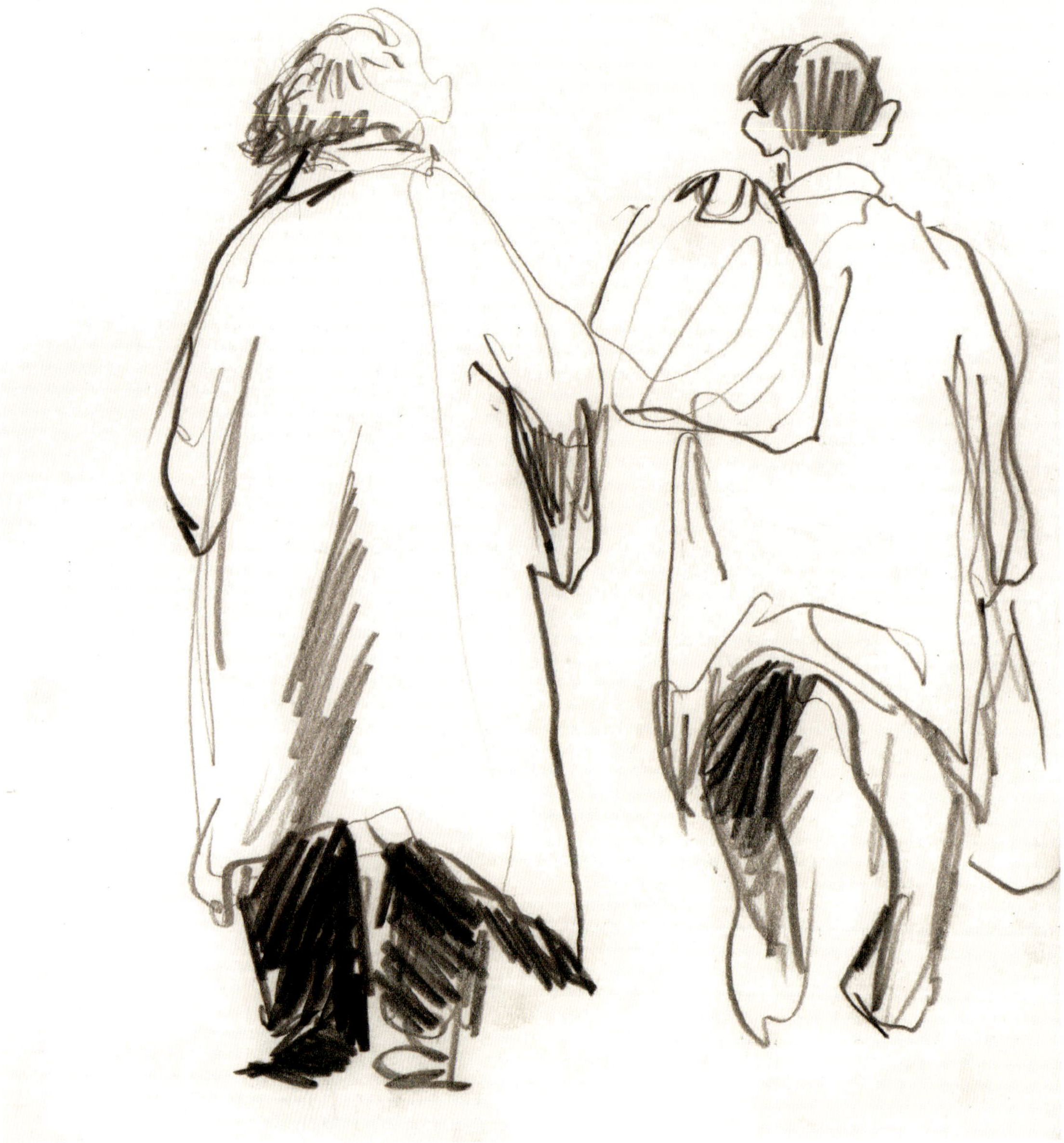

Going Home

I am a stranger on earth; do not hide your commandments from me (Ps 119:19). 'It is an old belief and it is a good belief, that our life is a pilgrim's progress—that we are strangers on the earth, but that though this be so, yet we are not alone for our Father is with us. We are pilgrims, our life is a long walk or journey from earth to Heaven.' Vincent van Gogh [*The Complete Letters of Vincent van Gogh* 1. Little, Brown & Co. 1991, p87]

List of Images

VISIBILIA series, no. 2
This first edition, limited printrun of 1000 copies

PO Box 83, Carlisle, CA3 9GR, UK
www.piquanteditions.com

Photography of artwork: Jesse Boles

British Library Cataloguing in Publication Data

Gabankova, Maria
Body broken - body redeemed : the art of Maria Gabankova
1. Gabankova, Maria 2. Human beings in art 3. Redemption in art
I. Title
759.1'1

ISBN-13: 9781903689141

PIQUANT editions

Design: Jonathan Kearney
Cover images: *Self-Portrait—My Hand* and *The Cross* by Maria Gabankova